MW00480328

# TO RESTORE

# EARTH'S

# BALANCE

## AWAKENING
## AN ALREADY~KNOWING

# TO RESTORE

# EARTH'S BALANCE

## AWAKENING

## AN ALREADY-KNOWING

(Finding Earth-Based Wisdom in
Indigenous Languages)

*Milt Markewitz & Ruth L. Miller*

Portal
Center
Press

Published by Portal Center Press, LLC
Oregon, USA
www.portalcenterpress.com

*ebook ISBN: 978-1-936902-39-2*

this print edition ISBN: 978-1-936902-40-8

# Dedication

To those people in my life whose voices I carry with me, and whose actions continue to inspire. Specifically, my father Arthur Markewitz, Rabbi Aryeh Hirschfield, and my colleague Kenneth Roffmann, all of whom have passed away. And to the rest of my family, my son and daughter Scott and Krissy, my grandchildren Julien, Devon and Sophie, my brother David and late sister Carol, and of course my mother Sophie. – *Milt*

To all those who are open to reawakening their already knowing and discern a glimmer of truth from which they begin a quest for yet more profound truths – particularly the generations that folllow and move forth with a sense of forgiveness as they clean up the mess we've bequeathed them. – *both of us*

.

# Table of Contents

Foreword..................................................................................................... i
Foreword..................................................................................................... vii
Introduction "What Have We Wrought?'............................................ 1
  An Historical Perspective ................................................................. 1
  An Ethical Shortfall........................................................................... 1
  The Earth as a Living System ........................................................... 2
  Our Work.......................................................................................... 3
  An Approach...................................................................................... 4
  A New HOPE .................................................................................... 5
1 Historical Perspective...................................................................... 7
  Empire-based Culture's Colonization............................................. 8
  Devolution......................................................................................... 9
  Our Reverse, or "Inside-Out," Culture........................................... 14
2. Ethical Shortfall............................................................................. 17
  Imam Toure's Message - Milt........................................................... 17
  Devolving from All-Life Consciousness......................................... 19
  A Conversation on Principles & Doctrines - Milt.......................... 21
  Understanding Where We Stand in Our Faith Traditions.......... 23
  Applying Guiding Principles............................................................ 24
  Games of Life .................................................................................. 25
3. Earth-based Consciousness............................................................ 29
  Getting Over Colonization............................................................... 31
4. Living Languages............................................................................ 35
  Awakening Our Deepest Knowing................................................... 35
  The Power of Ancient Hebrew ......................................................... 36
  Every Hebrew Word is a Story - Milt............................................... 38
  The Binding of Isaac (Yitzhhaq)...................................................... 44
  Shamanic Languages ....................................................................... 45
5. Building Bridges ............................................................................ 47
  Expanded Realities........................................................................... 47
  The Panarchy Process....................................................................... 49
  Panarchy in Language....................................................................... 52
  The Power of Story .......................................................................... 56
  Is Anyone Listening.......................................................................... 57

Teaching Stories - Milt..................................................57
A Living Systems Point of View............................................58
Experiencing the Shift - Milt..........................................59
Mechanical & Living System Comparison.....................60
Education for Learning.....................................................61
Paradigms for Sustainable Living.................................64
The Shift Exercise............................................................68
Living Systems in Our World................................................70
Living Applications - Ruth..............................................70
Systemic Understanding.......................................................72
Spiral Dynamics....................................................................73
Bringing Life to the Matrix.............................................75
The Concept of Chaord........................................................76
6. Toward A Culture of Connection.......................................79
Discovering & Learning........................................................79
Transformative Learning Experience – Milt...................79
Building Community.............................................................81
Appreciative Inquiry – Milt.............................................81
Transforming a Membership Organization with A-I – Ruth..... 88
Honoring Ways of Knowing.................................................91
The Human Dynamics Model..........................................92
Human Dynamics and Cultural Differences...................94
Achieving Consensus............................................................97
Releasing the Pain of the Past.............................................100
Ho'oponopono.................................................................101
Forgive Aught Against Any – Ruth................................102
Rediscovering Our Deepest Truths......................................104
Telling Our Stories – Milt...............................................105
Acting on Principle...............................................................108
Goals or Principles?.........................................................108
Learning & Teaching............................................................112
Pedagogical Comparisons—Milt.....................................112
The Ebb and Flow of Tribal Education...........................114
Ceremony.............................................................................118
Sun Dance—Milt..............................................................118
7. Hope.....................................................................................125
A False Sense of Hope.........................................................126
Sustainability........................................................................128

An Ancient Way of Thinking............................................129
Hero's Journey................................................................132
8. Moving Forward...........................................................135
Plans & Processes..........................................................137

Appendix.............................................................................141
The Binding of Isaac........................................................143
Ruth's Process.................................................................148

More Useful Links & Resources..........................................153

Gratitudes – Milt................................................................155

About the Authors..............................................................157

# Foreword

by Milt Markewitz

*The present disintegration of the life systems of the Earth is so extensive that we might very well be bringing an end to the Cenozoic period that has provided the identity for the life process of Earth during the past sixty-seven million years. During that period life expanded with amazing fluorescence prior to the coming of the human.*

*~ Thomas Berry & Brian Swimme[1]*

Our first book, *Language of Life: answers to modern crises in an ancient way of speaking,* had two major points. First was the description of the ancient Hebrew language as a language of life – an Earth-based language that was lost and needed to be recovered. The second was that Earth-based peoples who have retained their languages intuitively know all that's necessary to create and sustain our ever-renewing, flourishing planet.

Although it's only been 7 years since we published *Language of Life,* a great many changes have occurred—some favorable and many not. Just prior to its publication, I met the founders of the Indigenous Indian Institute, Nancy Maryboy and David Begay, and I told them the gist of what Ruth and I were co-authoring. David, who is Navaho, listened without speaking, and before we finished I asked him if he had any thoughts or feelings he'd like to share. He said, "Milt, when we speak our language it's like awakening an already knowing." David's words gave me a most important glimpse into his culture, and have resonated with me in almost every conversation about language since, whenever an Indigenous 'knowing' is shared, and most recently it came to mind when I recognized that the success in making the sort of paradigm

---

[1] Thomas Berry & Brian Swimme, *The Universe Story,* 3/11/94, p. 3

shift we're advocating requires 'awakening an already knowing' in ourselves.

Another important informant to our process is Ilarion Merculieff. I had never met Ilarion until the morning of a colloquium that is described in this book, in which he offered a completely new (to me) approach to Climate Change, and I feel very blessed to have done so. He is now my mentor, colleague, and friend, and has influenced and patiently supported my journey.

Our society's current solutions for addressing Climate Change and its related crises are almost all technological, and have obscured the many ethical shortfalls that underlie our ongoing conflicts, social injustices, and climate change. They ignore the unwillingness to give up our attachment to conveniences, comforts, and privilege that have grown exponentially, and are often thought of as rights. And they disregard the academic understanding of the attributes and endowments of all living systems that are well-established among researchers but generally absent from Western curricula, although when they are taught, awaken an already, though heavily obscured, knowing.

The *Curve of Hope* that we articulated in that first book must be re-examined critically to understand why it didn't materialize, and we need make the adjustments to actualize that curve. Climate change—a process described in many Earth-based prophesies and now agreed with by Western scientists, has been on an exponential destructive path for generations, with insufficient human response. What we offer here, then, is a path we might follow to create the viral shift we believe is necessary to create a *Curve of Hope* that results in humanity living in ecological integrity and communal harmony.

This new book assumes that we are facing an urgent situation in which:

→ only a handful of years remain to make the necessary significant changes to our current Modernity culture if humanity is to avoid decimation, and

→ those of us who were born and raised in this culture have neither the ethic nor tools to deal with the very difficult, inevitable consequences of what we've wrought.

A list of assumptions that I developed several years ago will serve as guiding ideas for this new book. They are:

1. Our Western Modernity culture has institutionalized not being sustainable.
2. Our desired state is one of a dynamic homeostasis — balance and harmony in a changing environment.
3. A change in Western consciousness is required to achieve that — a consciousness based on an ecological integrity that, among other things, leads to social harmony and equitable economics.
4. Current individual and collective technological actions are shifting Western consciousness incrementally in that direction; they are necessary but not sufficient.
5. That desired state is understood and well-articulated by many Eastern and Indigenous peoples, who have lived it for thousands of years.
6. There may be a way to integrate elements of Western Modernity into an Earth Based framework that maximizes the wellbeing of humanity for generations to come.

These guiding ideas tell us that humanity's collective work must be to recognize that our Modernity consciousness needs to be replaced by a radically different understanding of who we are and how the world works.

At first, shifting consciousness seems like an impossible task, but there are two basic saving graces, both having to do with the fact that what we are shifting to is a consciousness that has already been lived. The first is that its essence is still alive and being practiced by Earth-based cultures all around the world, and the second is that the consciousness we are shifting to is grounded in basic truths about life that, to varying degrees, already exist in every human heart, and are being awakened in people throughout the world.

The flow of this book will follow a paper I wrote in 2019 entitled, "What Have We Wrought", which is mapped into a Hopi prophesy that tells us that if we embark on a change in consciousness and wish to return to the old consciousness, we must embrace the essence of the original consciousness first. We must then accept that we're not in control of the overall process; the response to what we've triggered is controlled by Nature. Still, there's a possibility to address the challenges we face; we may still have time to reverse what we've wrought.

This book will therefore emphasize opening our hearts and minds to listening and learning from those cultures who've lived sustainably for millennia to address the current crises in our world. As we listen and learn, it becomes clear that we're only getting a glimpse of Earth-based cultures. That then leads to deeper listening, a growing trust in their relational ways, and an acceptance of their relational leadership — even as we continue to live and work in the world our Western culture has created.

We will be using the technology that has emerged in the past few years to create what is intended to be far more than a book— it's the first step in an implementation process for re-achieving ecological balance and communal harmony in the world. The next step is creating Earth-oriented embodiment experiences, through which our intent is that gradually, but with exponentially growing numbers, there will be a paradigm shift within the Modernity cultures so that humanity will once again know, and live from the understanding, that this beautiful, supportive planet Earth was given to us in balance and harmony, and it is our job to keep it that way by understanding and adhering to Natures' processes.

To launch this process we're using something called *100% Consensus*, the protocols for which are very similar to the Talking Circles used by Indigenous peoples for collective decision-making—to which our colleague Jeff Goebel has added some very insightful inquiries. Leading, and to a lesser degree, participating in the *100% Consensus* process requires a relational way of being that comes from embracing all life and valuing every opinion—essentially, doing things in an Earth-based way. The focal *100% Consensus* inquiries are:

- ✓ What is the situation? How do I feel about it?
- ✓ What are my worst possible outcomes of the situation if I try and fail?
- ✓ What are my worst possible outcomes of the situation if I do nothing?
- ✓ What are my best possible outcomes of the situation?
- ✓ What beliefs/behaviors/strategies/actions will foster the best outcomes?

They have been demonstrated to begin a different kind of dialogue—one in which the people participating begin to see themselves and the world around them in a new way, and from there begin to be able to work harmoniously for their individual and collective wellbeing.

This book is therefore an extension and expansion of what was written in our first book into something much more: the basis for an ongoing process. While those portions of the original book that are relevant and still valid have been included and modified as appropriate, the new material is based on what we've learned since.

# Foreword

By Ruth L Miller

When Portal Center Press approached Milt to prepare a 2nd edition of the book *Language of Life: answers to modern crises in an ancient way of speaking*, we thought he would take a look through the book, make a few changes, maybe add a new chapter or two, and move on. But no. Milt had learned a lot in the years following the original publication, and the world had continued on its exponential curve toward the decimation of the human population, so he couldn't simply re-issue what was said seven years ago and move on.

So, instead, he not only put together a whole new set of insights and understandings to be shared, but launched a new project: a *Listening* to the voices of the Earth-based peoples and to the understanding that is inherent in their languages which supports a living-systems consciousness and encourages a dynamic balance within this biosystem we call Earth. He called people from many cultures together to learn Jeff Goebel's *100% Consensus* process, which has proven itself so effective in bringing diverse groups into alignment as to how to maximize their individual and collective well-being. He developed graphic models to help us understand our real relationships with each other and the natural processes of Earth. He outlined a multi-pronged approach to creating experiences that can let people embody those essential understandings—so we now have an internet presence as well as both ebook and print editions of this text.

And we are happy to participate in this process, because he's right. Humanity has very little time to act, and whatever actions we take must be from a very different consciousness, a very different sense of who we are and how our lives relate to the planet we live on. And, while it is possible to begin to understand all that through years of study, a direct experience of a living-systems perspective can almost instantaneously shift individuals and groups from Modernity consciousness to the consciousness of harmony and balance that has sustained Earth-based peoples for millennia.

This book, therefore, is something new, introducing something as old as humanity: the experience of life as if we humans were part of it, rather than dominating it—and of relating to each other and the planet as if we were the interlocking pieces of the whole system of being that we are.

# Introduction
# 'What Have We Wrought?'

by Milt Markewitz

*They shouldn't be studying the animals;*
*They should be studying themselves.*

*~ Ilarion Merculieff, Unangan/Aleut Elder[2]*

## An Historical Perspective

The quote above is a partial answer to the question, "What have we wrought?" The context for such a question is the belief that there was a time 4-6 thousand years ago when a significant change in consciousness occurred for a growing minority of humans on the Earth. Nature was no longer the sole mentor for their learning and so it was the beginning of patriarchal Empire. Some time, probably just before Empire was the life of Abraham that subsequently created the Judeo-Christian ethic.

In short, the planet's soon-to-be most powerful peoples lost their connection to the Earth, and with that their deep understanding of being both relational and appreciative. Hierarchy became the primary organizing principle in every major institution: government, business, education, family, and religion. The Earth became a commodity through property ownership – on its surface of land and water, as well as the sky above and the minerals below.

## An Ethical Shortfall

With the advent of written scriptures, a new 'truth' was formed, that included humankind's "domination" over all other

---

[2] Ilarion Merculieff, Unangan/Aleut Elder, in his video, "Asking the Right Questions"

life forms, even though the accurate translation of that part of the book of Genesis sets Earth as man's dominion (as in realm, or property)—it does not say humanity gets to dominate other beings. Sadly, even people were commoditized when they were categorized as sub-human or condemned because they were unlike the "dominating" minority or failed to accept the new "truth."

In recent conversations, we seldom meet anyone who doesn't believe that there is an ethical problem underlying our current dilemma of wars, climate change, ravaging of the Earth, and social harmony issues. Considering this, we ask "Isn't it reasonable to assume that understanding *what we have wrought* requires that we look at ourselves individually and as cultures so that we might acknowledge our ethical shortfalls and correct them?"

## The Earth as a Living System

The relatively recent (when compared to the 67 million years during which the current life renewing processes emerged and the 200,000+ years that humanity has been known to walk the planet) 'Empirical' beliefs on which our culture is based obscure the understanding of the Earth-based peoples. Their beliefs say that all living systems, including the Earth itself, go through processes by which they cleanse, heal, and restructure so as to flourish. They teach that all such systems are designed for the emergence of something beyond their current structure; they are endowed through creation with life functions that are both nurturing for and experienced by human beings.

This wisdom underlies a wholistic, systemic understanding: that the Earth will always provide for its component beings, that, as long as we meet our mutual responsibility to respect and nurture all life, it will provide a *sufficient abundance*. It underlines the ongoing relational processes that could be expressed as the Natural Laws of Interdependence.

These understandings of many Earth-based peoples is both enhanced and reinforced by the living languages they speak. Like the Earth, many of these people and their languages have been ravaged thru colonization, racism, and exploitation, and like many species, many of the peoples and languages are now extinct. Yet those who remain and practice the ancient ways seem to intuit all that's necessary to create and sustain life—they manage to survive and even thrive. This requires a broader view of reality than the Newtonian view discerned by most in the Modernity cultures, more like a reality that's both Newtonian and Quantum, and perhaps, ultimately, mystical. Thus there's a broader spiritual connection within Earth-based peoples' language than in that of Modernity culture, which informs all words and actions. And this means that the organizational work described in this book be spiritually driven.

The essence of the Earth-based consciousness is choosing to live by uncompromised principles of ecological integrity, spiritual connection, and social harmony. Contrast this with our Modernity culture that compromises spiritual connection, ecological integrity, and social harmony with almost every individual and organizational economic decision.

### Our Work

Our work, therefore, is to recognize the poverty of our Modernity consciousness and replace it. The Earth-based wisdom-traditions model seems to be an appropriate replacement, but a major problem with such a replacement is that Modernity consciousness is grounded in religious beliefs of dominion, 'truth', commitment to dogma, and has built structures designed to protect and defend those beliefs.

Because of this, building academic and intellectual bridges, such as learning what differentiates a living system from a mechanical system, are fundamental. Defining spiritual pathways such as ceremonial experiences for healing and reconciling are essential. We will also have to understand the interdependent relationships of the processes applied by Earth-based peoples to their environments in such a way that future improvements will be accomplished—not by blending Earth-based ways into the ways of Empire, but by incorporating some effective Empirical ways into an Earth-based framework.

## An Approach

Addressing this paradigm shift in the brief amount of time left to reverse the exponential destruction we've caused, as made most evident by the current experiences of Climate Change, must take all of these into account. Our suggested approach is:

1. Call out to all people who agree with, or have a listening for, the need to develop a new consciousness based on Earth-centered ethics to participate in listening and learning from and with those people whose cultures have lived in balance and harmony for generations.

2. Convene Native and Eastern peoples and ask them to host ceremonial gatherings for all humanity to experience healing, reconciliation, systemic understanding, sufficient abundance, sense of place, languages, community, day-to-day survival, cooperative economics, Native sciences, and living by mutually agreed-upon guiding principles. Here we rely on Native leadership to develop the process and content, and ensure the effort is spirit-driven.

3. Build on all current efforts to examine Modernity culture's unethical ways of operating by convening religious leaders and encouraging them to look beyond current dogmas that obscure who we are and how the world works, for the well-being of Earth and of future generations. Two primary organizing bodies for such an effort are

   a. *The Parliament of the world's Religions*
   b. *The United Religions Initiative*

All of the above will require the use of various modern communication technologies to create succinct messages with widespread distribution.

And as in so many emergent processes, a fourth activity has come to the fore: we need to expand on the bridges that have already been developed to help us. We need to:

→ understand Living Systems and how they inform us of necessary paradigm shifts;

→ start using Talking Circles that help us understand how to Listen and Learn;

→ use forms of Decision-Making, that include Blending Apparent Opposites, and Relational Leadership;

→ recognize the power of Ceremony and the wisdom of Native Science and other principles that Earth-based peoples intuit and teach their children, but which Modernity culture has obscured.

## A New HOPE

The dominant societies within Modernity culture generally believe that technology is our greatest hope, but based on both academic research on the geophysical and ecological systems of Earth and a deep listening to the wisdom of Earth-based peoples, our understanding is that technology is necessary but not sufficient, as it leaves us with the same underlying ethical—hence behavioral—dilemma. Modern and emerging technologies are necessary because of the urgency and severity of our problems; we have a few years at best to reverse the centuries-long processes that have destroyed so much of the planet by ignoring ecological and communal guiding principles. They are not sufficient because *any real hope for humanity lies in rediscovering and basing our actions on ancient truths of living in balance and harmony with the life-renewing processes* bestowed upon all life millions of years ago, and then flowing with Nature.

# 1 Historical Perspective

*In these prophetic times, where human beings are pushing the Earth Mother's life support systems to the brink, it is imperative to do whatever is possible to elevate human consciousness.*
*We must heal separation from self, from other and Mother Earth. This separation is the root cause for all the human dysfunctions that are destroying Mother Earth and ourselves.*

*~ Ilarion Merculieff, Unangan/Aleut[3] Elder*

The geological evidence tells us that our planet Earth was formed as the $3^{rd}$ planet from our Sun approximately 4.5 billion years ago, and that the earliest forms of life appeared about 1 billion years later. According to Father Thomas Berry and Dr. Brian Swimme in their book, *The Universe Story*, life processes that are in place today began 67 million years ago in what has been labeled the Cenozoic Period. For the last 200,000 years human life in various forms has existed, and for almost all of that period Nature was the sole mentor for all humans.

When Milt mentioned to Unangan/Aleut Elder, Ilarion Merculieff, that he thought there was a profound change in human consciousness after which humans no longer exclusively relied on Nature, Merculieff agreed. And when Milt asked him how long ago that shift took place, he said "about 4-6 thousand years ago." According to archeologists and historians, this timeframe coincides with the formation of empires and the earliest Abrahamic traditions in the Asian-African region called the Fertile Crescent.

At that point the planet's soon-to-be most powerful peoples became urbanized, or "civilised," and so lost both their connection to the Earth and their deep understanding of being both relational with and appreciative of Earth's processes and

---

[3] Merculieff's people prefer to be called by their own name for themselves, *Unangan,* rather than *Aleut,* the name the Russians gave them a few hundred years ago.

gifts. Hierarchy became the norm in all relationships, the Earth became a commodity to be controlled and exchanged, and expansion of power through acquisition and control became a cultural expectation everywhere these people moved from that initial starting point: down the Nile River into Africa, across the deserts to India and China, and across the mountains into Europe.[4]

### Empire-based Culture's Colonization

Outside of the constantly-growing empires, those peoples who remained connected to the Earth continued to discern the value of all life, and lived their lives in accordance with principles of ecological balance and communal harmony. Often they struggled to maintain these ways when colonization, spurred by Empire culture's religious doctrines and governmental policies, included genocide and prohibition of many of their cultural norms.

Qualitatively speaking colonization has been very cruel. It has subjected Indigenous peoples through slavery, genocide, banning the speaking of their languages and performing spiritual ceremony, taking their land, and imparted diseases, sometimes intentionally to peoples with no immunity. Throughout the Modernity culture based on those initial empires, the cruelty continues as it's been codified in laws, imbedded in systemic racism, and in the false hopes that continue to draw individuals away from downtrodden reservations into urban life.

Quantitatively, colonization has been devastating. It's estimated that as many as 145 million people lived in the western hemisphere in 1491, before Europeans discovered them. By 1691, the population of those indigenous Americans had declined by 90–95 percent, to around 15 million people across the hemi-

---

[4] For a detailed description of this process see Miller's *Mary's Power*. For a simplified analysis if the impacts on our life today see Miller's *Discovering A New Way*.

sphere.[5] The following graphic shows how the numbers of those who have maintained their Earth-centered ways, based on Nature as their mentor, have dwindled, leaving few remaining to help us restore a balanced life by re-creating an Earth-based ethic.

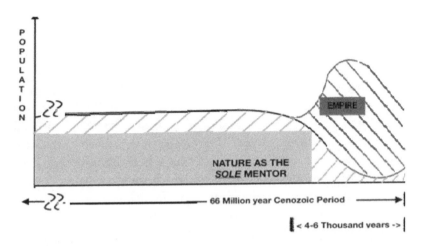

One of the issues that becomes clear from this graphic is that 4-6 thousand years is like the blink of an eye when compared to the length of time of the Cenozoic Period or even the time that humans have existed—even though it seems a very long time for people living today who don't have this sort of perspective and assume things have "always been this way."

## Devolution

The Empire culture has long taught that power-over and control are inate desires and actions among human beings, but seeing what we're doing to Earth and to each other as "just normal human behavior" leads to the fatalistic view that we are unable to change. It's an easy way to avoid trying to change.

Behind this belief, however, is a deeper awareness that could become an alternative belief: that we are continually evolving, and

[5] McKenna, Erin, and Scott L. Pratt. 2015. American Philosophy: *From Wounded Knee to the Present*. Bloomsbury Books. p. 375.

that for the past several thousand years we've been experiencing, not the continuous improvement we've seen in our material lives, but rather an intellectual and spiritual devolution.

Several Indigenous peoples have recognized these devolution processes and they've developed prophesies that have long told of the coming of this day of reckoning. Two such prophesies come from the Hopi people of southwestern North America, and they are integral to our finding a new consciousness and possible pathways for getting there.

For context, it's important to understand that the Hopis have lived in essentially the same location for at least 3000 years, and maybe longer. Their name describes them as "the people holding the world together in peace." Other North American natives call them "the oldest tribe" because they have been here so long. They farm the land around the mesas on which their towns are located as they always have. Their clans and families have criss-crossing lineages that they can trace for many generations back in time.

*In spirit and in ceremony, the Hopis maintain a connection with the center of the earth, for they believe that they are the earth's caretakers, and with the successful performance of their ceremonial cycle, the world will remain in balance, the gods will be appeased, and rain will come.[6]*

In their stories and traditional beliefs, the Hopi lived in other places before they finally settled on this spot in our world. They consider this world, or stage in their culture's life, to be the Fourth, the First World having been destroyed by fire, the Second by ice, and the Third World by floods. They were finally led to this Fourth World by their deities, known today as *Katcinas.*

*Since time immemorial the Hopi people have lived in Hopitutskwa and have maintained our sacred covenant with Maasaw, the ancient caretaker of the earth, to live as peaceful and humble farmers respectful of the land and its resources. Over the centuries we have survived as a tribe, and to this day have managed to retain our culture,*

---

[6] Emily Benedek, *The Wind Won't Know Me: A History of the Navajo-Hopi land dispute,* 1992

*language, and religion despite influences from the outside world.7*

So with all this in mind, the fact that there has been a story handed down for generations describing the modern world and the Hopis' role in it is worth paying attention to. One piece of the story has to do with the interconnectedness of all the people of the world. As the story goes, the Creator made four pairs of stone tablets and gave one pair to each of the races of humanity: Brown, Black, Yellow, and White. The tablets described how to live well in this world; it was a gift of the Creator to ensure that humanity would thrive. The Creator then sent the four races to the four continents, saying the time would come when they would be re-united, and that, as long as the tablets were not broken, their coming-together would be a time of joyful celebration, but if any of the tablets was broken, there would be strife and distress.[8]

Another part of the prophesy told them that when the "gourd of ashes" (uranium-based weapons, like the atom bomb) was dug up from under the ground near their homes (where it belonged and was safe) the world would suffer and the Hopi would have to instruct the nations of the world, who would come together in "the micah tower by the great water." This was, of course, the glass-faced building in New York city that does, in fact, sit by the bay and house the United Nations. So, at the space and time described in the prophetic story, the Hopi people sent a representative to the United Nations—in the 1980s and again in the 1990s—to explain to the nations of this world what would happen in coming decades if they did not stop living the way they were living, including rising seas, increased storms and earthquakes, and more wars.

---

[7] https://www.hopi-nsn.gov/ (official website of the Hopi tribe)
[8] "People of the Book", Jews, Christians, and Muslims, will immediately recall that when Moses brought the tablets from the Creator down from the mountain and saw that the Israelites had abandoned his teachings and turned back to worshiping an idol, he threw the tablets down in anger and smashed them.

Part of that prophecy is depicted in a simple rock carving at a sacred site near the Hopi villages. Willie Whitefeather, a Cherokee story-teller, found this so important that he created a film called HOPE[9] to help everyone in the world understand it. Briefly, it describes "everyman" as evolving to the point where he has a choice: follow the path of Earth-based simplicity, symbolized by the stones and the corn plants on the lower line, or follow another, apparently higher, path where lots of people live close together and have lots of things.

Taking the upper path with lots of people is very attractive for a while but becomes very "bumpy" with lots of ups and downs and, ultimately, comes to an end, requiring a return the the lower path—that of Earth-based simplicity.

In the film, Whitefeather shows how our Modernity culture has been built on the pain and blood of many peoples, how difficult it is to sustain, and how many disasters must result, until people

---

[9] Find Whitefeather's YouTube video here: https://youtu.be/lVSmLpNK45Q

wake up and restore their spiritual connection with each other and the Earth. In the Hopi story describing the carving, the end of the bumpy path is the end of what we're calling Modernity culture, and all that remains of humanity at that point will, by necessity, end up living a simple life of reapiing Earth's abundance and living creatively in harmony with Nature.

The following graphic explanation of the stages in these Hopi Prophesies begins with the consciousness recognizing that "all earth systems are alive and earth is our sole mentor", and flows through the devolvement process and the infusing of authentic Earth-based wisdom into modern cultures.

**LIVING THE HOPI PROPHECY**
Milt Markewitz – May 20, 2020

No problem can be solved from the same level of consciousness that created it.
Albert Einstein

**Ethical Shortfall**
*Wars, Social Injustice & Climate Crisis*

**Creating Bridges**
*Living Systems, Cultural Comparisons, Paradigm Shifts, Living Languages*

**Hierarchical Institutions**
*Business, Religion, Education & Governance are all Un-Sustainable*

**Resonance Deep Inside**
*For some it was obscured, for others it was a glimpse of a reality*

**Separation From Earth**
*Developed a Human Centered Consciousness*

**All Earth's Systems are Alive**
*Nature was our sole Mentor*

**Can only Accurately Convey the Consciousness we've Lived**
*Those who've experienced, embodied, and practiced life processes*

**Reconnect with Life**
*Nature as Primary Mentor for learning life's relational processes*

**Infuse Earth Wisdom**
*Valuing all life, Ecologic, Communal, Principled, Systemic, Spiritual, and Grateful*

**Authentic Partners**
*Connect with local Tribes, Native schools, and support Organizations*

It then flows through where we are today, building bridges that begin Awakening Our Already Knowing, recognizing that Earth-based consciousness can't be conveyed by those who haven't lived it, and following a set of steps so that all humanity can adopt the Earth-based ways with integrity, and so thrive for generations to come.

## Our Reverse, or "Inside-Out," Culture

Indigenous teacher Ilarion Merculieff calls Western, empire-based, Modernity cultures 'Reverse Cultures', and says the sequence for the reversal began with our disconnection from Earth, 4-6,000 years ago, when we moved into cities. Ilarion tells us that his Elders now call us the "inside-out" cultures—an apt description of who we have become, with our focus on what is around us, rather than our inner being.

One way to understand what has happened to the peoples of the earth is illustrated in the graphic, below.

Originally all humans were deeply connected and learned from Earth

Colonization rapidly reduced the number of Earth based people, whole tribes, and their languages

Adoption of Western ways further eroded Indigenous cultures. Sovereignty was lost and Indigenous mores were ridiculed.

Now there are relatively few tribes and individuals whose wisdom transcends the pain, value all life, and live by ecological and communal guiding principles.

Separation occurred 4-6K years ago.

We attempted to travel in parallel paths.

Dominating cultures abused collaborative processes and the agreements they produced.

The cultures continued to diverge as they lived by very different guiding principles including appreciation for life.

**How might we adopt and adapt life's flourishing ways and travel in truly parallel paths?**

The start of Empire and the Abrahamic Faiths

Domination of other species and humans became a dogmatic belief.

Hierarchal replaced relational as a primary way of organizing

As winning replaced consensus, military might, power over, and wealth became paramount.

Much of Earth's life is now threatened, all stemming from our separation 4-6K years ago.

While empire-based cultures have spent the past several thousand years developing amazing technologies in the material world, we have, at the same time, been devolving, socially and spiritually, into this "Reverse Culture." Stark examples of this reversal can be found in every major institution, as well as the choices we make as individuals: from the way our children are taught to the way our elders are "warehoused," from the way we see ourselves and others as so often "less than" to the way we ignore the intrinsic value of the natural world that gives us every breath we breathe, every stitch we wear, and every cell in our bodies.

This "upside-down" way of being came about through some very explicit acts as well as more subtle compounding actions. Some of the explicit acts contributing to our current situation are:

→ an intentional disconnection from Earth,
→ codification of humanity as dominating over all other beings (in both the Hebrew Old Testament and the Christian New Testament),
→ continued acquisition and control of "new" (to us at least) lands,
→ formation and maintenance of hierarchical relationships and organizations.

Through separation and domination, we have lost the balance between men and women, youth and elders, and diverse peoples, as well as any appreciation for all life. We have let harmonious relationship be subsumed by hierarchy, dismissed ecological and communal guiding principles, and ravaged Earth for personal and corporate gains. Perhaps the most severe effect of our separation has been the loss of our inborn covenant with all other life, and the mutuality that exists for cooperating with and stewarding one another. Finally, our inner 'knowing' has been replaced by a dogmatic 'believing' that is codified into law and our national identity.

Yet there's hope. As people listen to and learn from those Earth-based peoples who honor all life, follow life-affirming guiding principles, and are deeply connected with their spirituality through ceremony, many who were raised in the colonizing cultures have discerned a sense of a Heaven on Earth not unlike that described in the first book of the Hebrew Bible, *Genesis* and again John's *Revelation*, the last book in the Christian New Testament. For these people, the possibility opens up that

Empire-based Modernity culture may be destroying a heavenly way of being which all life has been gifted.

## For Reflection

Seeing the world and our experience in this way is a big shift from what which we were taught in our Empire-based Modernity culture. Please look at Ilarion Merculieff's 3-4 minute video, "Asking the Right Questions" and ask yourself,

> ➢ What have we wrought?
> ➢ Shouldn't we be studying ourselves?

# 2. Ethical Shortfall

*Does not the sacred thus humanized fall under Jesus' curse:*
*'Get thee behind me Satan: thou art an offence to me:*
*for thou savourest not the things that be of God,*
*but those of men?'*

*~ Carlo Suares[10]*

Our understanding of the above quote is that only goodness exists within Creation and that the essence of all life that emanates from Nature is pure, while what is "of men" is dangerous at the least. In this context, there is only one type of suffering—that imposed by humans. What we consider to be suffering based on those acts of Nature we call 'natural disasters' might be better understood as the planet cleansing itself (and us) to re-establish balance and harmony. And the grief we feel when something we love is lost can also be understood as a deep appreciation for whatever or whomever was loved, dampened by the knowing that it is no longer available directly to us, since it is being returned to the Earth in an ongoing emergent, nurturing process.

Reading the New Testament in this way brings us in closer relationship with both the people of Jesus' time and the Earth-based Indigenous people of today.

### Imam Toure's Message ~ Milt

In November of 2017 Ilarion Merculieff facilitated a gathering described as follows:

*As humanity stands at a crossroads, 13 Indigenous Elders from diverse cultures around the globe gathered in Hawai'i to discuss the state of the world and invited the filming of their councils and ceremonies to co-create a message for humankind.[11]*

---

[10] Suares, Carlo. *The Cipher of Genesis: The Original Code of the Qabala*, Weiser, 1992, p. 11.

[11] The video may be found here: https://www.wisdomweavers.world/

The message that was born in that meeting may be critical for survival of the human race, so their plan was to translate the proceedings into several languages, one of which was Arabic.

Ilarion called to ask if I knew of any Arabic translators. I told him I would ask some Sufi colleagues who are leaders in the mystical branch of Muslims. So I asked a Sufi Imam, who told me that he couldn't help because he only new Arabic as a language of the Koran, not conversational. He referred me to other another Sufi leader, but we couldn't find a 'right' person for the work. Finally, I called Imam Momadou Toure, of the Bilal Mosque in Portland, with whom I'd worked on several interfaith projects, and he not only said he'd help with the translation, but related the following

> When I have an issue that requires spiritual inspiration, I turn to the Koran, just as you might turn to the Torah, or a Christian might refer to the Bible, but an Indigenous person seeks an understanding from Nature.

He later told me that there are three pillars of Islam: the Koran, the practitioners, and Nature. The former is thought of as most predominant and Nature is largely omitted.

Imam Toure's comments opens up many questions, among them:

→ Might this be true of all the Abrahamic traditions, and other Modern religions?

→ How did this shift from Nature to dogma take place?

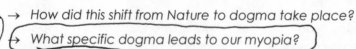

→ What specific dogma leads to our myopia?

→ What specifically have we lost that has us not knowing what we don't know?

→ Mightn't it be reasonable to assume that understanding Nature can lead us closer to the 'truth', and/or to the acceptance of mystery that makes 'truth' elusive?

Both authors of this book have done extensive interfaith work, and often there's a gathering of people of different faiths who share their scriptures and stories, looking for commonality and the comfort it brings—feeling the truth that we're not so different as we were led to believe. Doing so, people find our common humanity, but not generally our connection to all life.

Too often, then, coming together in such a way obscures the work that really needs to be done, which must be exploring our own responsibility, even culpability, in the ethical problems of Modernity culture. So here we are, offering a way to go beyond the commonality in our religions to discover the commonality of life shared by all beings.

## Devolving from All-Life Consciousness

If, once again, we look at the last line of Merculieff's quote, *"This separation is the root cause for all the human dysfunctions that are destroying Mother Earth and ourselves,"* we can see how empire-based cultures formed cities and states—that separated individuals from Earth, and how the incremental changes resulting from that shift compounded into our current world situation.

Looking beyond the actions to the underlying doctines, dogmas, and justifications for this culture's commodification of all forms of life, we begin to see, as well, a continuing ethical shortfall. The challenge to deal with that shortfall is to look at ourselves in the context of our upbringing and what we were taught that led us to our current beliefs.

As an example, one of this book's authors, Milt, is Jewish, so he looked at specific examples of when the Jewish People:

→ Lost our Earth-based Ancient Hebrew language

→ Lost our connection to the Universe – our cosmology

→ Embraced being hierarchical

→ Compromised guiding principles

→ Failed to discern humanity's interdependence with all other living beings

→ Became colonizers

→ Became colonized

From answering questions like these, he has developed his own story, in the context of his religious upbringing and current affiliation. As a result, he's more in touch with his own culpability, as well as his connection to the commonly held Jewish stories, and he can more clearly discern how he wants to change his own story and the story of his people.

Ruth grew up without the doctrines of a specific religious tradition, but was immersed in the dogma of Science—which has, for several decades, become a form of religion in western Modernity culture. In her studies she learned that in the 1600s Fr. Rene DesCartes proposed the separation of the natural sciences from understandings of the mind and spirit as a way to end the battle between the Roman Church and those who studied the Earth and stars; Fr. Francis Bacon defined the scientific method about the same time; soon after, Rev. Isaac Newton developed his method for measuring gravity, light, and heat. Since then, scientists have attempted to understand Nature by analysing every little bit of the natural world, carefully ignoring the possibility that spirit or mind might have a role in what was being observed. As a result, throughout the twentieth century, Science

→ Defined life as a mechanical process that can be taken apart and understood piecemeal

→ Assumed that humanity is separate from natural processes and can control them

→ Operated as if each individual can be understood apart from its surroundings and background

→ Offered a model of the past and future in which material expansion was the ultimate goal

→ Set up a series of "have to accomplish" requirements for any individual to be considered a worthy contributor to humanity's well-being

Living from this model of life led to significant material progress for the empire-based cultures, but also caused significant disturbances in natural processes. For Ruth, personally, it led to significant health challenges, which, ironically, the sciences could not address. It took a series of actions based on spiritual traditions

*[Handwritten margin notes: "Philosophy of scarity and theology of abondance", "Historical separation of spirit & science led to this pg", "Reconnection of science & spirit return of", "to ERA"]*

to overcome those physical challenges which, then, opened up a whole new world of inquiry for her, based on the interconnectedness of mind and body, spirit and soul (which she later wrote about in other books and will be described in some detail later in this book).[12]

Both of the sets of doctrines we grew up with, and the cultural choices that led to them, are symptoms of a shift in consciousness away from connectedness and toward isolation, away from integration and cooperation toward separation and competition, and away from gratitude for abundant supply and toward fear and grasping over perceived scarcity of resources.

## A Conversation on Principles & Doctrines ~ Milt

When I was on the board of the Spiritual City Forum of Portland, our monthly lunch meetings featured a speaker, followed by a brief time for questions intended to stimulate dialogue at each table. Our program theme was to better understand the sustainability teachings of various religions. I invited a Jewish colleague who was studying Environmental Sciences, Shamu Fenvyesi, who I thought 'walked his talk' both as a Jew and a steward of the Earth. He agreed to share, and spoke eloquently of Jewish Law, the commandments, our covenant with God, and some of the scriptures related to our relationship with the Earth. He shared a Jewish story intended to alter our thinking by touching our emotional and spiritual core. And he spoke of Jewish ethics: our belief in 'original goodness' and the notion that there are constant, ongoing, ethical breakdowns that must constantly be repaired; how it is our responsibility to perform virtuous acts toward humankind and the Earth; and how it is a gift to perform these acts because they are all part of a virtuous cycle.

Shamu's talk was wonderfully received and the questions that were asked to stimulate the dialogue that would follow reflected people's appreciation. As the question period came to a close, a

---

[12] Ruth's healing experience is described in *Finding the Path, a healing journey*, WiseWoman Press, 2007.

gentleman in the back of the room asked, "How do you reconcile your humanitarian way of being with Israelis shooting Palestinians in their olive groves?" An uncomfortable silence followed his question as we proceeded into the small group dialogue portion of our program. When the luncheon was over, I asked the gentleman who had asked the difficult question if we could have coffee together, and we set up a date.

As the time approached, I felt as if I had to organize my thoughts well and in a non-argumentative way. And I decided to see if I could develop a construct based on guiding principles that stimulated a generative conversation. The graphic that follows, 'Archetypes of Religion', is based on the assumption that every religion has to one degree or another four basic guiding principles.

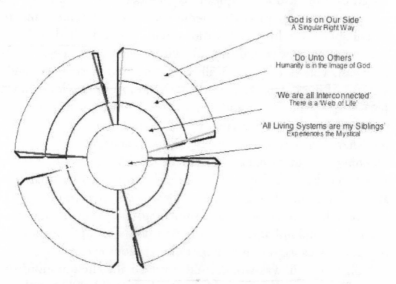

"ARCHETYPES OF RELIGIONS"

Each Slice of the 'pie' represents a Faith Tradition

The Circles are Guiding Principles found in all Faiths

'God is on Our Side'
A Singular Right Way

'Do Unto Others'
Humanity is in the Image of God

'We are all Interconnected'
There is a 'Web of Life'

'All Living Systems are my Siblings'
Experiences the Mystical

The graphic may be misleading in that each principle is drawn as a concentric circle, when, in fact, the degree to which one principle or another exists varies in each religion, but it worked for the purpose at hand.

In this graphic, the 'pie' represents any and all faiths, with each 'slice' being one faith tradition, and perhaps a slice for those who claim no faith at all. Each concentric circle represents a guiding principle that, as stated above, I believe exists to one degree or another in each faith tradition.

The gentleman I was meeting with, John Nichols, brought his wife Caroline with him. They are of the Baha'i faith. We explored the chart and each of us quickly concluded that Shamu, the speaker at Spiritual City Forum, was coming from the circle at the center of the drawing, his primary guiding principle being 'All Living Systems are my Siblings.' The Israeli shooting at Palestinians in their olive grove probably believed a literal interpretation of the Old Testament and thought that God had bestowed all of what is now the State of Israel to the Jewish People, and that therefore 'God was on his side.' What followed was truly a generative conversation, and I remain good friends with both John and Caroline.

## Understanding Where We Stand in Our Faith Traditions

Milt has used the above chart on many other occasions as a way of stimulating Inter-faith understanding and dialogue. Often the conversation reveals the belief that the outer circle has embedded in it a world view of 'scarcity'—win/lose, no sharing—while the inner circle has embedded in it a sense of 'abundance'—infinite in terms of love and blessings, embracing all life, and with humanitarian behavior being paramount when it comes to social justice. Also, it seems that each of us usually operates around more than one of the principles: one that we predominantly claim and a second that often strongly influences our primary principle.

The two guiding principles in the middle are perceived quite differently depending on how they are influenced by the outer and inner principles. 'Do Unto Others,' if most strongly influenced by the inner circle, elicits virtuous behavior, but if the influence is the outer circle it becomes 'an eye for an eye'. 'We are all interconnected' is somewhat the same, in that from an outer-circle perspective we perceive ourselves as a 'collection of objects,' but with an inner-circle perspective, we become 'a communion of subjects.'

There are groups of people, mystics, who live in the center circle of this chart. They often maintain a religious affiliation as they energetically connect with the Universe. They have generated a love for all life, demonstrating that our essential humanness supersedes any religious dogma, and the game of life, as they play it, is based around guiding principles.[13]

> There is a real difference between a commandment and a vow, especially as Buddhists understand the latter term. A commandment is an order levied upon one by a superior. A vow is a personal statement of intent. The former implies an enforceable hierarchy of power; the latter relies solely on your own integrity. [14]

The question becomes, then: how might we modify our most basic principles so their essence remains intact while guiding us to be in greater harmony with life?

## *Applying Guiding Principles*

Several years ago, Milt was asked to participate in a planning meeting for a conference to design the economic system that would be integral for a renewable world order. A group of the planners met for dinner the evening before the planning session was to begin. When Milt introduced himself, he told them where he was from and why he thought he was invited, and then he said,

> I know this is an economic conference that we're planning, but I wouldn't focus on economics. Instead I would concentrate on defining principles of ecological integrity and communal harmony, and then design the economic system so that it didn't violate those principles.

---

[13] For a helpful overview of the common inner core of major religious traditions, try *The Perennial Philosophy* by Aldous Huxley.

[14] Rabbi Rami Shapiro, *Minyan: Ten Principles for Living a Life of Integrity* Potter/Ten-Speed/Harmony/ Rodale, 2010, p. 45

There were three Indigenous people in the room and each commented their agreement afterwards. The understanding they shared is that, in our Modernity culture we don't have well-articulated ecological and communal guiding principles, so we have consistently compromised Earth and our social harmony because almost every decision we make is based on immediate, cash-based, economic advantage—as part of our "Reverse culture."

## Games of Life

The notion that all of life can be lived as one of two types of games, one with a rules-base, called 'finite', or one based on guiding principles, called 'infinite', is clearly articulated in James Carse's book, *Finite and Infinite Games; A Vision of Life as Play and Possibility.* Examples of related finite and infinite games abound. For instance in the legal field, litigation is a finite game while justice is an infinite game; in athletics, winning games is finite while sportsmanship is infinite; and in education, training is finite while learning is infinite.

In most cases, therefore, playing a finite game is part of playing an infinite game. In fact, one of Carse's most profound observations about the nature of these two types of games is that a multitude of finite games can be, and usually are, played within the infinite game, but the infinite game can never be played within a finite game; one must step outside the finite game's rules and norms to operate in the infinite. (An example is shaking hands across the net after a tennis match, which would be impossible within the rules of the game of tennis, but is a demonstration of the infinite game of sportsmanship.)

If this is true, it would seem axiomatic that you can't play the infinite games of 'global community' or 'diplomacy' under the finite game of 'the war on terror, ' but you can play 'the war on terror' under the infinite game of 'global community.' And, like the other infinite and finite games, focusing on the infinite game is probably the only way the finite game of 'the war on terror' can be won.

Similarly, our perception that we must play either the finite game of being the global superpower or the infinite game of being part of a balanced and harmonous world order needs to be changed so we can be playing both.

When games are played in empire-based Modernity culture, one side typically wins and the other loses. Very rarely do both sides win or both sides lose. But a question that Carse's book raises is, "What creates 'lose/lose' situations?" In the examples cited above, this would be participating in athletic events without a sense of sportsmanship, or entering into litigation without a sense of justice. This realization leads to the suspicion that 'lose/lose' situations occur when we are playing finite, 'win/lose' games without understanding the necessity of being governed by the guiding principles of the infinite game in which they are embedded, making it so that no 'win/win' situation exists.

One way, therefore, to understand what's happening today is that nearly everybody in Modernity culture is playing win/lose finite games in every facet of our lives, without adhering to guiding principles of the infinite game of social and ecological order. Such principles serve as indicators, a sort of 'ethical compass,' and when we get 'off course', there are serious consequences.

In Modernity culture the tendency has been to label the consequences of our own actions as problems to be solved. We disregard our part in creating the situation, ignoring the principles of the infinite game we're playing, and this very framing of our efforts leads to creating more 'lose/lose' outcomes. Without realizing the need for the principles associated with the infinite game we are really playing, we can only experience more "lose/lose" situations, with the associated distress for all involved.

This is at the heart of Modernity culture's ethical dilemma. Our interminable conflicts, social injustices, and climate crisis are all the consequences of win/lose games and, without a deep commitment to living by guiding principles of ecological integrity and communal harmony, they can only devolve into lose/lose scenarios.

"not good enough" restricted my spirit due to negative

### For Reflection

Think about a time when you realized that what seemed at the time a very deeply held belief didn't serve you well.

➤ How did you alter your belief?

➤ What were the consequences – benefits and difficulties?

➤ What are the important considerations to reflect deeply on before embarking on a change in a deep belief?

➤ What specific dogma leads to the sense that you are separate from Nature?

➤ What specifically have you, and the folks around you, lost that has us not knowing what we don't know?

➤ What might this world be like if our culture didn't encourage us to think of Nature as something to dominate or control?

➤ What kinds of guiding principles might we be working along?

understanding of who I am – modernity child receptive therapy. Focus on EBC shifts understanding of my the child within –

# 3. Earth-based Consciousness

Fortunately, there are some cultures remaining on each continent whose people have lived in accordance with the principles of the infinite game, abiding by the Natural Law of interdependence for millennia. Inherent in their understanding is that we're all in this together; that all life includes all humans. They have attempted to share this understanding with empire-baed leaders and students many times over past generations, too often not being listened to. Yet when earth-based Indigenous peoples from diverse geographical locations are brought together, we find that they're able to connect deeply, and almost immediately, as they share their stories, customs, songs, dances and food. More, we see that there is a common, agreed-upon, Earth-based, wisdom to which they mutually adhere.

An example of both is documented in a video, *Yakoana*, which shows how, in a 10-day gathering prior to the 1992 Rio de Janeiro United Nations Conference on Development and the Environment, nearly a thousand tribal leaders from every continent developed extraordinary relationships through the sharing of their cultures and rituals built on their common concern for Mother Earth. From the deep trust and love that was created, and the sharing of their deepest of guiding principles for life, there emerged a Manifesto.

At the time, the Indigenous peoples of the world were given only 5 minutes on the conference agenda, and their spokesman, Marcus Terena, a native South American, organized the First world Conference of Indigenous Peoples to give them an opportunity to share in those minutes. The Manifesto they composed was essentially what he shared during his limited time, and at one point he said,

*This life code that no scientist has ever managed to unveil rests with the Indians. You don't have to look any further. Are*

29

*you prepared for that? Is the contemporary world prepared for what we want to convey after 500 years?*[15]

It is absolutely astounding that peoples with no common language and from diverse cultures from all around the world could come together for such a short time and come up with a consensus on how to address the most significant challenge humanity has ever faced. (We think that part of why they could put this presentation together was that many of these cultures speak non-alphabetic languages, which we'll talk about in the next section of this book.) It is even more astounding that their message, as with so many before, hasn't been embraced by world leaders—it's been largely ignored by the government and nongovernment organizations who were at that conference ostensibly to find solutions.

This Earth-based consciousness goes well beyond those people who are considered Indigenous. If we listen to the Hindu, Buddhist, Shinto, Pagan, and some Western religious traditions, they, too, have maintained their connection to the Earth—at least in part. Regular, often seasonal, rituals that remind people of their dependence on the Earth's bounty for their own wellbeing, hymns recognizing that Earth's processes are part of the Good of Creation, and the maintaining of ancient Earth-centered traditional activities (like Irish Catholics walking up a hill in their bare feet to tie their prayers to a tree) that do not fit, but don't conflict, with the religious (or scientific) doctrine being practiced keep at least a small part of that sense of connection that we feel deep inside us somewhat in our awareness.

For Indigenous peoples, such seasonal rituals and ceremonies, hymns, and ancient traditional activities are the center around which daily life revolves. Food, clothing, house decorations, words spoken and sung, the contents of sacred spaces and sites—all are made and chosen to fit and support these ancient traditions that ensure balance and harmony among all living beings. Those peoples who live Earth-centered lives do so with every aspect of their beings, every day. From their first words

---

[15] Marcus Terena, First world Conference of Indigenous Peoples. Rio de Janeiro, 1992.

in the morning to the last words spoken or sung at night, they are connecting and reconnecting with All That Is. The Earth is the source of their material well-being and they know it. The Sun is the source of energy for the Earth and they know it. The Sky is the bridge between the two and they honor it for that.

They train people in their communities to sense the movement of animals, the variations in the climate, the balance of the people, and to guide the people in ways that maintain or restore the harmony of it all. They tell stories and sing songs for the children that make sense of everything they observe and experience as a single whole, created by Spirit for humanity to live in, enjoy, and become more fully who they can be.

Part of that process of guiding children is to help them gain access to a deeper wisdom, to what the Abrahamic traditions call "the voice of God or angels." As children are able, they're encouraged to sit quietly and listen—listen to the trees, the birds, the animals, and the people around them; listen to their own heartbeats and breathing; listen to the deep vibrations of the earth and water; listen to the faint whisper of a voice that is Spirit, perhaps coming in the form of an animal or plant, guiding them to develop their gifts and make their contribution to the community.

## Getting Over Colonization

In his book, *Wisdom Keeper: One Man's Journey to Honor the Untold History of the Unangan People,* Ilarion Merculieff documents the slavery of his people, first to the Russians who came to the Aleutians in 1741 in search of furbearing riches, and continued under United States government when jurisdiction over his People was transferred in the Treaty of Cession in 1867. Colonization was brutal, as genocide in several forms reduced their population; "Eighty percent of the Unangan were wiped out within 50 years of the Russian fur traders arrival."[16] And in addition to being slaughtered and subjected to diseases for which they had no immunity they were forbidden to speak their language, hold their

---

[16] Illarion Merculieff, *Wisdom Keeper, one man's journey to honor the untold history of the Uangan people,* PenguinRandom House, 2016, p. 7

ceremonies, teach their children, and gather or produce enough food to survive.

Ilarion tells the story of growing up in what was essentially a 'company town' where everything was doled out by the US government, and his father working up to 16 hours a day killing seal pups whose pelts were given to the oppressors for their profiteering. In 1963 this US travesty was revealed in an Alaskan newspaper, and in a matter of days the US pulled out of Ilarion's village on St. Paul Island.

Ilarion was a young leader at the time and knew that in order to rebuild his peoples' spiritual, fiscal, and communal health they needed to rediscover and strictly adhere to their Native Ways. This included restoring the balance between men and women, being relational in everything they did, including ceremonies, as well as how they listened, spoke, made consensual decisions, educated their children, used the valued opinions and traits of all their people, and flowed with Nature. They made a plan to enhance their harbor and in four years flourished fiscally, and so the culture was rebirthed and continues on its emergent path.

This story is most important, not primarily because they'll 'live happily ever after", or even because it's a model for survival that's badly needed and from which we can all learn, but because it helps us understand the traits on which all their actions were grounded.

These traits provide the synergism that bonds all the other ways of listening, speaking, decision-making, and application of science and education, as well as provides the basis for happiness, contentment, gratitude and bliss found in such cultures. They are shown in the following graphic as the Valuing of All Life, with each life having a unique value of its own, and living by un-compromised guiding principles of ecological integrity and communal harmony.

This chart is an interpretation of Ilarion's sharing of how everything needed to be done the Native way. Once grounded in the valuing of all life and the ecological and communal principles, then it's folly to think that we can take a facet of the Earth-based way of being, embed it in our empire-based Modernity way, and expect it to be understood or workable.

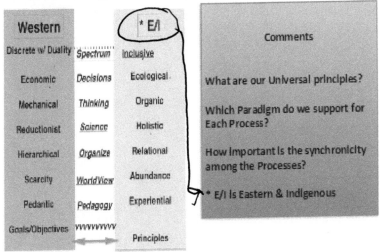

## Blending Consciousness

| Western | Spectrum | * E/I Inclusive | Comments |
|---|---|---|---|
| Discrete w/ Duality | | | What are our Universal principles? |
| Economic | Decisions | Ecological | |
| Mechanical | Thinking | Organic | Which Paradigm do we support for Each Process? |
| Reductionist | Science | Holistic | |
| Hierarchical | Organize | Relational | How important is the synchronicity among the Processes? |
| Scarcity | WorldView | Abundance | |
| Pedantic | Pedagogy | Experiential | * E/I is Eastern & Indigenous |
| Goals/Objectives | | Principles | |

Sadly, though, that's precisely what seems to be happening in Modernity culture. We borrow some facet of the Earth-based ways, like arranging seats in a circle rather than rows of desks or chairs, and think we've made the necessary paradigm shift. What we have in fact accomplished is: *we've gotten a glimpse and now need to dig deeper*. We basically need to rethink how we play the various "games of life" so we can be governed by guiding principles that flow from reconnecting with Earth.

## For Reflection

As you think about the stories you were taught as a child, can you find ones that taught you that Nature or the world was dangerous and needed to be controlled?

➢ Can you find ones that taught you that Earth sustains all beings?

> Can you remember songs or seasonal practices that connected you with Earth?
> Can you think of ones you've heard of other people doing that might have that effect?

# 4. Living Languages

*For today's scholars who search for meaning and 'truth' from the ancient texts, their monumental task will not lead them any nearer the Source, not only because the Bible is untranslatable but, strange as it may seem, because it is already hopelessly translated in Hebrew.*

*~ Greg Braden*[17]

According to Unangan/Aleut leader Ilarion Merculieff, all languages emanate from the vibrations of the Earth. Their understanding is that languages vary only because the vibrations vary from location to location, but the essence is always the same.

That may be why, when the Indigenous peoples of the world were given five minutes on the 1992 Rio de Janeiro Environmental Summit, they convened almost 1000 people from around the world and were able to share through stories, food, songs, and dances. As described above, they were able to bond into a very cohesive group, and in just over a week's time, develop their message to the United Nations summit and select their speaker.

Such a process is practically unheard of in Modernity culture, but it's one that the authors believe could be emulated—if the rest of humanity accepted the relational leadership of Earth-based peoples to guide us.

## Awakening Our Deepest Knowing

*Value change for survival.*

*~ Chief Oren Lyons*[18]

Here we are beginning the year 2021, more clearly understanding that we are faced with the most serious ethical dilemma humanity has ever confronted, addressing Climate Crisis.

---

[17] In the Foreword to *The Cipher of Genesis, The Original Code of the Qabala as Applied to the Scriptures* by Carlo Suarez.
[18] Faith Keeper, Onondaga Nation

It's a race we may have already lost. If we have a chance to survive, much less thrive, we need an ethical transformation.

Could our answer lie in the enlightened knowing and teachings that flowed more than 5000 years ago and are documented in hieroglyphics[19] that artistically display the essential meanings of the oral languages spoken by regional cultures? Could we awaken a deeper already knowing in the masses of humanity who seem to recognize our dilemma but don't know what to do or how to proceed?

Those people who have embodied Earth-based ways for millennia have many of the answers that we need, and we are ready for their voices to be elevated that we might accurately emulate their relational ways. Only then will we all begin to recognize that Nature's cleansing, healing, and restructuring processes are our best ally, and offer the hope we so badly need as we experience the consequences of our past actions. As we embrace the power of the Natural Systems of which we are a part, we will learn to once again flow with Nature. And we, the authors, are convinced that the power to do so lies in the languages used by Earth-based, indigenous peoples around the world.

## The Power of Ancient Hebrew

Our first book, *Language of Life,* recognized the ancient Hebrew language as a template for life for the Jewish people and the ethical basis for all the Abrahamic traditions that followed. That book was written in the recognition of the need for an Earth-based language to help us move forward through the crises of the 21st century, and the understanding that our Jewish ancestors once had, but have now lost the ancient cosmology and deep knowing exhibited by Earth-based cultures. In that book, therefore, we looked at the power of the ancient Hebrew language, based on its structure, sound, and deeper interpretations, as a cultural template for an Earth-based Judaism – the 'value change' to which we must return.

---

[19] We refer the reader to any online resource or traditional text regarding heiroglyphic writings in the andicent Nile valley.

The first written Hebrew is said to have been the stone tablets that were kept in the Ark of the Covenant.[20] Moses told us in Exodus 32:16 that the tablets he offered the tribes of Israel were the work of God, and the writing was the writing of God. He used the design of the 22 symbols on the tablets as an alphabet by giving them sound values. A few hundred years later, the energetic Hebrew aleph-bet he offered was transformed into the world's first alphabet.

The letters also have numeric values, such that the letter *aleph* also is used for the number 1, the letter *yod* is also used as the number 10, and so on.

From time to time we learn something so seminal that we feel we are experiencing a basic truth—it clarifies questions we hold about life, informs our way of thinking and being, and provides a framework for more profound learning. One such jewel, a 3x9 matrix of the ancient Hebrew language, is found in Carlo Suares' inspiring book, *The Cipher of Genesis: The Original Code of the Qabala as Applied to the Scriptures*.[21] In that book Suares combines the 22 basic Hebrew characters with the 5 characters that are called 'final' or 'sofit', which appear differently when they are at the end of a word, to form a 27-character system of letters.

The three rows of his matrix represent three distinctly different energies:

1.  an Archetypal nurturing process in the top row (single digit numbers),

2.  an Existential presence that is felt or sensed by all life including Earth in the middle row (double digit numbers), and

3.  the Cosmological Force that existed at Creation and continues to this day in the bottom row (triple digit numbers).

---

[20] Archeologists have found writings in a "proto-Hebrew" on the walls of Egyptian turquoise mines.
[21] The website www.natureslanguage.com provides more detail on ways to apply and understand Suares' matrix.

Together, the nine columns appear to be all that is necessary and sufficient to support all life processes.

| ARCHETYPAL, ABSTRACT WORLD | | | | | | | | |
|---|---|---|---|---|---|---|---|---|
| ט | ח | ז | ו | ה | ד | ג | ב | א |
| Tayt | Hhayt | Zayn | Vav Waw | Hay | Dallet | Gimmel | Bayt Vayt | Aleph |
| 9 | 8 | 7 | 6 | 5 | 4 | 3 | 2 | 1 |
| **EXISTENTIAL, NEWTONIAN WORLD** | | | | | | | | |
| צ | פ | ע | ס | נ | מ | ל | כ | י |
| Tsadde | Pay Phay | Ayn | Sammekh | Noun | Mem | Lammed | Kaf Khaf | Yod |
| 90 | 80 | 70 | 60 | 50 | 40 | 30 | 20 | 10 |
| **COSMOLOGICAL WORLD** | | | | | | | | |
| ץ | ף | ן | ם | ן | ת | ש | ר | ק |
| Final Tsadde | Final Phay | Final Noun | Final Mem | Final Kaf | Tav | Sheen | Raysh | Qof |
| 900 | 800 | 700 | 600 | 500 | 400 | 300 | 200 | 100 |

It should be noted that when Hebrew transitioned to an alphabetic language, it lost the energies described by the three rows, and the most important connection between our Earthly existence in the 2nd row and the cosmological Creation force of the 3rd row. This connection exists between the symbol for *Kof*, also representing the numbers 20 and 500; *Mem*, numbers 40 and 600; *Nun*, numbers 50 and 700; *Phay*, numbers 80 and 800; and *Tsadde*, numbers 90 and 900.

## Every Hebrew Word is a Story - Milt

Each letter-number in Hebrew can also be spelled out as other letter-numbers and thus carry those energies as part of their own. For example, the word for the symbol *Aleph* (א) is spelled *Aleph-Lammed-final Phay*, and so carries its own energy as a symbol, plus that of final *Phay*, which is Cosmological Energy, and *Lammed*, which is Existential Organic Life. And, of course, each of the 'secondary' letter-numbers is composed of 'tertiary' letter-numbers, e.g. *Lammed* is composed of *Lammed-Mem-Dalet*. The progression, and thus the infusion of energy, is never-ending.

When I shared the 3x9 matrix with a new acquaintance, Yvonne Vizina (Métis), who had been praised for her work with Indigenous languages, we talked about the energy of some languages being every bit as, or more important than, their vocabulary, and she began to cry. It was then that I realized the profound connections among peoples who speak the languages that emanate from Earth.

In *Language of Life* we articulated the impact of ancient Hebrew through examining several more words and the seven-day Creation story in the beginning of *Genesis* in the Old Testament.[22] Our assumption was, and still is, that the 9 Cosmological characters in the ancient Hebrew should be the driving force in the Jewish/Christian Creation story. As we look at a few Hebrew words below, the Cosmological characters will be highlighted by using a larger font.

The revelation came to me when I heard Mahatma Gandhi's grandson, Arun Gandhi, tell the story of going to his grandfather and asking him to explain peace. As Arun tells the story, the Mahatma gave his grandson a kernel of grain and sent him on his way. Arun put the kernel in a box and then forgot about it. Years later he remembered, and then asked his grandfather to explain the shriveled kernel. His grandfather said, "If you had placed the kernel in nurturing soil and watered it, it would have created its own seed, and with some work you could have had a whole field of grain."

I met with Arun after he told the story, and asked him if his grandfather was energetically connected to Sanskrit. I gave me a surprised look and said, 'Yes. Why do you ask?' I told him of my study of the Ancient Hebrew and my 'aha' moment when I

---

[22] Batya Podos contributed greatly to that part of the *Language of Life* book, for which we are truly grateful.

thought about the Jewish word for peace, *Shalom* **(Sheen,** *Lammed,* *Vav,* **final Mem)**, and how it tells the same story that his grandfather shared with him. The Cosmological *Sheen* and *final Mem* create the Archetypal capacity for fertilization, *Vav*, from which Existential organic life, *Lammed,* emerges. This is how it looks in this framework:

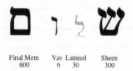

Final Mem    Vav  Lameed    Sheen
   600         6    30        300

Four Hebrew words exemplify the power of the language from four perspectives: *Shalom, Baruch, Eretz,* and *Radah.* It will help understanding if the reader remembers that, in Hebrew, words are spelled from right to left. We've already begun analyzing *Shalom.* Now let's look at the others.

*Baruch (Bayt,* **Raysh,** *Vav, final Kaf)* – the Hebrew word for Blessing or Blessed, and at first when I thought about it phonetically was these are the three characters in Suarez' *Perfect Order & Structure* column. How incredibly Blessed we are!! When I saw how it was actually spelled, I realized that what I thought was *Kaf,* because it's the last character in the word, is in fact a **final Kaf,** which is the Creation force for *Universal Life.*

Final Kaf    Vav    Raysh    Bayt
   500         6     200       2

My interpretation is that we are blessed with absolute perfect order that either exists when everything is biodegradable or when we assume that even our plastics and other materials are biodegradable over a very long period of time. I began to see how what we do on Earth by ravaging its structure has an energetic, transformational connection to a Natural process. In this particular case, the connection is to the Creative force of *Universal Life,* and Nature is doing what it must to cleanse and heal with the activities we call "Climate Change," and when they're severe, "Climate Crisis." Then, by including *Vav,* which stands for Nurturing Fertilization, the blessing is enhanced further as we discern Earth as a life support system.

*Eretz (Aleph,* **Raysh, final Tsadde),** is the Hebrew word for Earth, and the last word in the first sentence of Genesis, and like so many words in our Creation story, it has multiple Cosmological characters. Our Earth was defined by two Cosmological Forces, Perfect Structure, and Attraction or Love, and enhanced by the nurturing processes of the Life-Death-Life continuum.

Final Tsadde    Raysh    Aleph
900             200      1

Like the word *Shalom* and all other combinations of this energetic language, there's a story told that shapes the cultures that speak them, and also has the ambiguity so that the story-teller and the listener provide interpretation.

It has been interesting to share this word with folks from the Western culture who deeply believe that we're all interconnected, and feel affirmation because of the Attraction or Love that was given to us at Creation. Now love becomes far more than an emotion, it is a gift of life that perhaps underlies all our acts of ethical behavior – compassion, kindness and respect, the Indigenous peoples' valuing of all life, and operating in accordance with uncompromised ecologic and social guiding principles.

*Radah (Vav,* **Raysh,** *Dallet, Vav),* is the Hebrew word that means "realm" or "dominion."

# ו ד ר ו

| Vav | Dallet | Raysh | Vav |
|-----|--------|-------|-----|
| 6 | 4 | 200 | 6 |

As stated in the first chapter above, "Historical Context," the change in consciousness from an Earth- based to Empire way of being occurred 4-6 thousand years ago, and probably nothing has solidified our ravaging of the Earth as much as this translation of a passage in Genesis, written about that time:

> And God said, 'Let us make man in our image,
> according to our likeness; and let them have dominion
> over the fish of the sea, and over the birds of the air,
> and over all the wild animals of the earth, and
> over every creeping thing that creeps upon the earth.'
> ~ *Genesis* 1:26

Since ancient Hebrew is a living language that continuously reminds all its speakers and listeners that all life is endowed with the Creation blessings, it doesn't seem reasonable that any one life form is in the sole image of God. Moreover, domination is a concept that's not inherent in Nature, since the Creation processes are both interdependent and in place so that all life might flourish. The idea of domination was developed long after the *ancient Hebrew* was lost. The word in the Torah for Dominion is *Radah*, with the cosmic force defining Perfect Order and Structure and Birth with its inherent resistance, enclosed on both sides by Nurturing Fertilization. It's describing how the Earth flourishes, and that's our *Dominion,* the realm in which we and all life forms are continually renewing! There's no word for Domination in a language based on life energies. The mistranslation seems therefore to be a product of Empire with its assumptions of hierarchy and power over.

Not coincidentally the Hebrew word that is most driven by Cosmological characters is the first word of *Genesis* in Torah (the

Old Testament), B'reishit, (*Beyt,* **Raysh**, *Aleph,* **Sheen**, *Yod,* **Tav)**. The three Cosmological characters: *Raysh*, meaning Cosmological Order and Structure; *Sheen*, Cosmological Life (the breath of G\*d[23]); and *Tav*, Cosmological Birth. Together they create the Archetypal processes—*Beyt*, Order and Structure; and *Aleph*, the LifeDeath-Life Continuum—that are necessary to support *Yod*, the Existential Life-Death-Life Continuum.

Perhaps there are other Hebrew words with 3 Cosmological characters, but as you can see in the words chosen above, having two and sometimes just one Cosmological character gives a strong, energetic force to several key words. What may be coincidental, but it's doubtful, is that there is a potential word with 4 Cosmological characters: the word Christ, **Qof, Raysh, Sheen, Tav**.

Each of the words above makes a specific point. Take a moment, please, and think about how each word changes your perception regarding the power of Earth-based languages.

→ *Shalom* – exemplifying how every word is a story.

→ *Baruch* – where we discern transformation as characters are energetically connected across life processes.

→ *Eretz* – how differently we feel when *Love* is a field of attraction among all life.

→ *Radah* – when a different translation powerfully shapes culture – sometimes detrimentally.

→ [Christ?] **Qof, Raysh, Sheen, Tav** – when a revelation of the highest order is obscured by previous expectations.

When we realize that a language, any language, can have this many layers of meaning and power, and look at the relatively simple understanding we gain from our own—then consider the number of languages that are currently spoken in the world (a quick Google search suggests that there are close to 100 languages that are spoken by over 10 million speakers and several thousand

---

[23] Because Torah says not to speak the divine name, the Jewish people don't even write the word fully, so the * is used instead of the letter o.

spoken by a few thousand speakers)[24]—we begin to see that there may be an untapped wealth of understanding and capability there.

## The Binding of Isaac (Yitzhhaq)

In *Language of Life* we articulated the impact of ancient Hebrew on its speakers and their environment through examining several more words and the seven-day Creation story in the beginning of *Genesis* in the Old Testament.[25] Our assumption was, and still is, that the 9 Cosmological characters in the ancient Hebrew should be the driving force in the Jewish/Christian Creation story.

We also included Milt's interpretation of "The Binding of Isaac" from this new understanding of the language, and what emerged was a very different story. It wasn't about G*d[26] asking Abraham to sacrifice his son, but rather a story of revelation and the creation of the Jewish 'DNA' that would be carried on in all the descendants of Isaac. (See the Appendix for a copy of this alternate interpretation of the story as printed in *Langage of Life*.)

This means that what you may have previously understood as a story about a father being commanded to kill his son is, when we understand the language as an Earth-based, shamanic expression, more a story about revelation and the test of adversity to assure a successful birth and perpetuation. Today some of the essence of the understandings gained by Yitzhhaq have been retained and some lost. What has been retained manifests in ethical behavior, and in beautiful connections with life that give the sacred places in life the feeling of deep love and caring. But there are strong cultural forces that impel us into act in ways that will deeply harm, perhaps even kill, future generations: our children. From this perspective, the "Binding of Yitzhhaq" is a very relevant story for our times: each of us must find our own

---

[24]https://en.wikipedia.org/wiki/List_of_languages_by_number_of_native_sp eakers

[25] Batya Podos contributed greatly to that part of the work, for which we are truly grateful.

[26] We're honoring the Jewish commandment not to speak the name of the Creator in the traditional manner of Jewish texts.

way to revelation, and to be tested so that we develop our tensile strength and sense of courage.

## Shamanic Languages

One of Milt's colleagues, Dr. Matthew Sheinin, expressed what may be the most powerful realization when he saw the Ancient Hebrew matrix, "This opens up the possibility of discovering what we don't know we don't know."

Is it possible that language illuminates the compelling powers at the core of all we know? Mightn't this be what Milt was feeling as he explored the Ancient Hebrew, or Yvonne Vizina's tears when she connected Suarez' 3x9 matrix to her own experience with language, or David Begay's comment, "Milt, when we speak our Navaho language, it's like awakening an already knowing"?

Hebrew, as used today, is no longer an Earth-based, shamanic language—the characters exist as letters but their energy and meaning has been lost. Also, the ancient oral tradition has been largely replaced with the written word. As a result, we've lost the capacity for deep understanding that the language originally held. We read the *Torah* as if we know it is Truth, but the Truth has been obscured by written words that lack energy, and, paradoxically, the ambiguity that is necessary if the stories are to retain their essence. Virtually every scripture has lost its original meaning, and the problem perpetuated when our interpretations are developed without the wisdom imbedded in the ancient Hebrew. "The Binding of Yitzhhaq" is one very small example of what's been lost.

It's essential for humanity's future well-being that we recognize that there are many cultures that have retained their shamanic, Earth-based language, and that emanating from their language is a deeply held sense of life being in harmony and balance, as well as an appreciation for all life yielding a profound happiness.

## *For Reflection*

Contemplating the power of the letter/sounds in the words used in the book of Genesis:

> ➤ Could these Cosmic Creative forces of the Life-Death-Continuum, Organic Life, Perfect Order and Structure, and Birth, be the essence of Christ consciousness?
> ➤ Is this a story that's been obscured in Modernity?
> ➤ Could this powerful Indigenous language, with this most powerful word, illuminate our connection to life and be the spark around which the world-wide Interfaith community agrees on what we wish to become?

Understanidng that there are things we don't know we don't know requires some reflection, often followed by 'aha' moments. For some it will come from a feeling, for others thinking, and ultimately may require an embodiment exercise.

> ➤ What questions do you have regarding what you don't know?
> ➤ Would you like to know more about quantum reality, communicating with other life forms, mutual responsibilities, 100% consensus, generational widom, and other topics?
> ➤ What's your mode of learning?
> ➤ Where might you turn to have the experiences you desire?

# 5. Building Bridges

It has become clear that when the fundamental vitality of our surroundings is embedded in our language, then we develop an accurate intuitive understanding of this world and our place in it. If it is not, then we probably need to develop educational bridges[27] to these ways of learning and knowing. This is a primary shift in worldview, or paradigm that is critical to the survival of our species.

Some of our ethical awakening will come from religious transformation, but as Ruth described in her experience above, many people in the western Modernity culture don't have a religious affiliation. We believe there are several bridges that could facilitate the Transformative Learning we've come to understand is necessary for dealing with the crises arising from Modernity culture's ethical dilemma. These are:

1) The expanded sense of reality that comes from an understanding of the processes we call quantum mechanics;

2) The sense of interconnectedness that comes from an undertanding of the structure and dynamics of living systems;

3) The awareness of cyclical flow through time that comes with an understanding of the processes of panarchy and spiral dynamics.

## Expanded Realities

In Gary Zukav's, *The Dancing Wu Li Masters: An Overview of the New Physics*,[28] he tells the story of observing quantum phenomena

---

[27] www.appreicativesustainability.com offers workbook materials for these ideas.

[28] Gary Zukov, *The Dancing Wu Li Masters: An Overview of the New Physics*, William Morrow, 1979
https://www.amazon.com/Dancing-Wu-Li-Masters-Overview/dp/0060959681

with several other physicists, and when trying to explain to him what they saw, the English speaking physicists said, 'The problem in trying to explain what we've just seen is we don't have language to describe it.' A Chinese physicist responded, "We do; it's *Wu-Li*."

There are two characters each for the Chinese words *Wu* and *Li*, and multiple interpretations contribute to an understanding of the phenomena they describe. The term "*Wu Li*" can mean "patterns of organic energy," which is a nice way to think of quantum mechanics. It also means "nonsense," "my way," "I clutch my ideas," and "enlightenment," which all apply, as well. And so Zukav organized his book around multiple interpretations.

The quantum reality Zukav describes in his book is exemplified in Ilarion Merculieff's, "Being Present,[29] a must see 3-4 minute video, in which he opines that birds exist in "a field of total awareness," a field that is available to all life and necessary for his people's survival. As he states, "One won't be a good hunter unless s/he connects with the energy of the animal being sought." When Milt framed a question to Ilarion about this connection in terms of what he believed, he said "this isn't a belief; it's a knowing."

Another westerner, David Peat, listens, learns, and collaborates with Blackfoot Indian scientists like Leroy Little Bear as well as many tribal members in his book, *Blackfoot Physics.* The following summary is written on the back cover.

> *What becomes apparent is the amazing resemblance between indigenous teachings and some of the insights that are emerging from modern science. Peat's insightful observations extend our understanding of ourselves, our understanding of the Universe, and our place in it. This book is a captivating read for anyone interested in the relationship between science, spirituality, and different ways of knowing.[30]*

---

[29] http://www.nativeperspectives.net/loadvid.php?watch=NUI6tUCtY28
[30] F. David Peat, *Blackfoot Physics, A Journey Into the Native American Worldview,* Phanes Press, 1995.

For many people in Modernity culture reality is based on the Newtonian physics that is the visible, replicable science available to people in our materialist way of thinking. Based on what Earth-based people are saying, our connection to a broader science may have been our biggest loss when western culture entered cities and separated from Earth. We seem to have lost our understanding of what quantum physicist David Bohm called the *implicate order*[31] of the Universe and our Earth—we no longer sense that which underlies and sustains the visible, tangible forms we experience.

Western scientists have caught up to a degree, but haven't seemed to affect the teaching in our schools, or the knowing of our ethical leaders, much less the general population. They have not yet discovered how badly we need to embrace Earth-based relational leadership and quantum intuition to guide our journey out of the mess our culture has created.

*a form of governance that would encompass all others.*

## The Panarchy Process

The book, *Panarchy: Understanding Transformations in Human and Natural Systems*, is authored by C. S. "Buzz" Holling and several colleagues, each of whom studied a large natural system, such as reefs, savannahs, and glaciers. They would meet periodically to compare notes, and they found that all the systems they studied follow a common pattern of flow.

As illustrated in the graphic below, the cycles can be expressed in terms of an idea becoming an organization, an acorn becoming an oak forest, or any other living system achieving its full potential. In all of them a seed begins to take root, and as it does so it builds relationships with other elements of its environment. Those relationships become more and more complex, and as they do so, new structures are formed. Over time those structures become more and more fixed and inflexible. At some point, then, one of the constant inputs of energy or information from the environment is too much for the now-inflexible system to manage—it experiences a Catastrophe, and

---

[31] David Bohm, *Wholeness and the Implicate Order,* Routledge, UK, 1980.

Chaos ensues. How long and how intense that Chaos becomes is a function of the capacity of the members of the system to let go of its old structures and allow a new seed to take root.

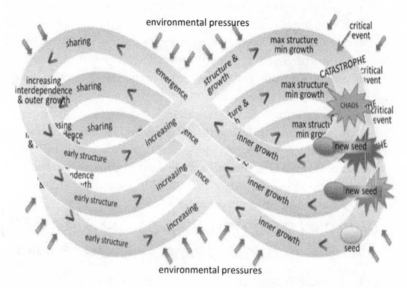

We can see this process in the way a young, green forest or meadow experiences fire, or the way a company deals with changing technologies, or the way an individual deals with life's transitions.

The following graphic is a simplified version of researchers' findings and illustrations that can provide ueful insights into both the flow and potential interventions.

In order to analyze the never-ending Panarchy cycle, begin with the lower right quadrant, in which an "External Force," or activating energy "awakens" and nurtures latent seeds and immediately leads to "Release" of energies and form. Moving into the upper-left quadrant, "Reorganization" activities allow the integration of new structures and possibilities. The process then moves to the lower-left quadrant, where gathering in surrounding resources ("Exploitation") make it possible for the system to be fertile and integrate other forms of life.

## Single Loop Panarchy Cycle

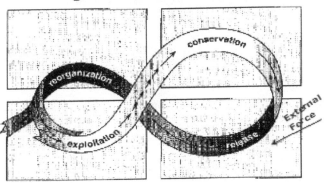

The system moves into the upper-right quadrant, a near-dormant stage of stability and structure ("Conservation"). Then, once again, an external force leads to the release of new, latent seeds of possibility and form, and the cycle continues.

Each cycle is driven by energy and transforms that energy into another energy that perturbs the system and leads to other cycles—all within the same Release, Reorganize, Exploitation and Conservation pattern. Thus the individual cycles of *Panarchy* are nested into an infinite number of cycles, all contributing to the continually self-organizing living system that is our world.

These cycles describe all living systems. They are geological, like eruptions and earthquakes; epochal, like forests and lakes; annual, like our seasons. They can be as short as nanoseconds, in the case of particles, or can take billions of years, in a star system.

It's also sometimes not at all what we expect. Holling tells of being one of the first people to be on Mount St. Helens a few months after it erupted in 1980. His expectation was that he would see devastation and death everywhere, but instead he was seeing the beginning of new life, all around. We can all discern examples of this process in Nature, and, since we are all a part of Nature, we can see examples in our own bodies and lives—at work, in community, in education, and virtually everywhere we experience interdependent activity.

We can apply this model to human cultures overall, as well. People arrive in a new environment with a vision of what's possible and begin to establish norms of interaction with each other and their surroundings. Initially, they work with what they have, but very quickly they begin to exploit their surroundings for resources that make it possible for them to flourish. Once they have reached a level of ease and comfort, they find ways to replenish those resources and maintain their communities in a balanced, harmonious way, unique to their physical environment and initial assumptions about who they are and how the world works. Cultures like the Hopi, who embrace this process, can flourish in the same locations for thousands of years.

The Panarchy model also explains systems that don't flourish, helping us understand more clearly why. Where *Exploitation* continues to the point where essential resources become scarce, or when *Conservation* leads to structures that impede the flow of energy and information, both of which are the norm in our empire-based Modernity culture, we recognize a failing system. If we look at what distinguishes these failing systems from those which succeed, we realize that assumptions of power-over, with their prevailing activieis of acquisition and control, prevent the emergence of a thriving cultural system.

## Panarchy in Language

Even languages, and the emergence of ideas within and through them, reflect this pattern. For example, a simple application of Panarchy to ideas is to map the energy of a single Hebrew character (e.g *Sheen*) the bottom loop, and then combine it with other energetic characters to make a word (e.g. *Shalom*) in the middle loop, and then tell a story in the upper loop that is interpreted in different ways by the teller and the listeners and ultimately become part of shaping individual thinking and perhaps establishing cultural norms.

This capacity of language to shape an idea and lead to cultural norms—was explored by anthropologists Benjamin Whorf and Howard Sapir in the 1930s and is known as the "Whorf-Sapir hypothesis."

Based on observations of peoples' activities and having evaluated descriptions of how the world works from many different cultures, they noted that the structure of the language individuals are taught from birth affects the structure of their mental processes, beliefs, assumptions, and logical train of thought.

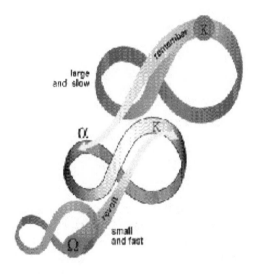

Whorf's *Language, Thought and Reality*[32] provides insights into the relationship between the structure of one's initial language and later experiences. He provides an example from the Hopi culture that illustrates the point, explaining that their language includes 7 different verb forms, or aspects, that have to do, not just with time, but with the space, location, and medium in which the action occurs. He also points out that these forms allow one basic verb stem to be modified into many very different uses and meanings, for example:

---

[32] Benjamin Whorf, *Language, Thought, and Reality*, MIT Press, 1956.

| | |
|---|---|
| *wa'ya* | *makes a waving shake (like a small tree shaken)* |
| *ya'ya* | *makes a sway from one side to the other* |
| *pi-'ya* | *makes a flap like a pair of wings* |
| *ta'ya* | *makes a racking shake* |
| *yo'ya*<br>*in an arc)* | *makes a circuit (axial turning combined with advance* |
| *ro'ya* | *makes a turn or twist* |
| *ri'ya* | *makes a quick spin* |
| *waya'yata* | *it is shaking* |
| *pi-ya'yata* | *it is flapping wings* |
| *yaya'yata* | *it is swaying* |
| *yoya'yata* | *it is circling round and round* |
| *roya'yata* | *it is rotating* |
| *riya'yata* | *it is spinning, whirling*[33] |

Whorf goes on to suggest that this use of many verb forms become the basis for the Hopi experience of the world, and their ability to function in it:

> *All this has a wider interest than the mere illustration of an aspect-form. It is an illustration of how language produces an organization of experience. We are inclined to think of language simply as a technique of expression, and not to realize that language first of all is a classification and arrangement of the stream of sensory experience which results in a certain world-order, a certain segment of the world that is easily expressible by the type of symbolic means that language employs. In other words, language does in a cruder but also in a broader and more versatile way, the*

---

[33] Benjamin Whorf, "The Punctual and Segmentative aspects of verbs in Hopi (1936)" in *Language, Thought, and Reality,* MIT Press, 1956. Reprinted in Google Books:
https://www.academia.edu/36270267/Language_thought_and_reality_selected_writings_edited_and_with_an_introd_by_John_B_Carroll_foreword_by_Stuart_Chase

> *same thing that science does. We have just seen how the Hopi language maps out a certain terrain of … physics.[34]*

More recent studies, using functional brain scans and other newer technologies, have confirmed that one's original language determines, to a significant extent, the way the brain is structured and how it works, and therefore how an individual views self and the world, and interacts with others. A 2019 article in the prestigious journal *Science* summarizes the results of such studies:

> *…a growing body of research is documenting how experience with language radically restructures the brain. … speakers of different languages develop different cognitive skills and predispositions, as shaped by the structures and patterns of their languages. Experience with languages in different modalities (e.g., spoken versus signed) also develops predictable differences in cognitive abilities outside the boundaries of language. … Even seemingly surface properties, such as writing direction (left-to-right or right-to-left), have profound consequences for how people attend to, imagine, and organize information.[35]*

Other recent research, especially that described by Joe Dispenza,[36] has shown that it is possible to modify patterns of interaction in the brain, thus altering the basis for our thought and experience. In his books and workshops he provides specific instructions for undoing past thought patterns and replacing them with new ones that permit a different world-view:

> *When you learn new things and begin to think in new ways, you are making your brain fire in different sequences,*

---

[34] Ibid.

[35] Lera Boroditsky, "Language and the brain" *Science* 04 Oct 2019: Vol. 366, Issue 6461, pp. 13.DOI: 10.1126/science.aaz6490. https://science.sciencemag.org/content/366/6461/13#:~:text=Language%20p lays%20a%20central%20role,how%20we%20make%20moral%20judgment s.&text=Further%2C%20speakers%20of%20different%20languages,and%2 0patterns%20of%20their%20languages.

[36] Joseph Dispenza, *You Are the Placebo, Breaking the Habit of Being Yourself,* and numerous video presentations and workshop recordings.

*patterns, and combinations. That is, you are activating many diverse networks of neurons in different ways.*

*...To break free from the chains of hardwired programming and the conditioning that keeps you the same takes considerable effort. It also requires knowledge, because when you learn vital information about yourself or your life, you stitch a whole new pattern into the three-dimensional embroidery of your own gray matter. Now you have more raw materials to make the brain work in new and different ways. You begin to think about and perceive reality differently, because you begin to see your life through the lens of a new mind.*[37]

Understanding that this is so—that our worldview is set, in part, by the language we speak, and that both the language and the structure of the brain can change—is part of why we, the authors, are writing this book. We are convinced that more of us need to have the embodied experience of the power of an Indigenous language to help us see, and know, the world in a different way—a way that enables us to act and react in way that is harmonious with Nature's processes, which, after all, are essentially supportive of the well-being of all living systems, including us.

This knowing that emanates from Earth and becomes integral to cultural wisdom is conveyed through language. Through the language it affects every facet of the culture—the sense of emergence, relationships, systemic understanding, and connection to all life, which in turn affects the science, education, spirituality, governance, survival, and who we are for Earth and community.

## The Power of Story

Because stories formulate some of our deepest beliefs, and the stories being lived today by the most influential individuals, corporations, and nations of Modernity culture aren't sustainable; we must do whatever we can to create new stories. In the words of the Ecuadorian Achuar People when asked by the North

---

[37] Joe Dispenza, *You Are the Placebo*, Hay House, 2013, pp.47-51.

*[margin handwritten note: why change is difficult and why it's vital to understand & speak nature]*

American founders of the Pachamama movement what it will take for the planet to become sustainable:

*We must change the dream of the North.*[38]

Implied in such a statement is an understanding of both the dream that we are living and the dream to which we must transform, as demonstrated in the Hopi Prophecy described above.

## Is Anyone Listening

*If a tree falls in the forest,*
*and there's no one there to hear it,*
*did it make a sound?*

Indigenous peoples have been telling us about their lives, beliefs, and knowing for generations. Some have been heard and touched peoples' hearts; others have been largely ignored or dismissed. As a result, for the most part, people haven't known how to act when the voice inside them tells them there is a deeper truth about life.

Then, too often, when they hear Indigenous people share their stories, they don't know how to respond to that inner voice that the stories are awakening. Sometimes they try to retell the stories they've heard, but when they do, they lack an authenticity. Indigenous stories must be told by those who have lived them.[39]

## Teaching Stories ~ Milt

The Spring of 2020 I was scheduled to teach an 11-week class on sustainability for the Columbia Gorge Community College in Hood River, for which I had lined up Indigenous facilitators to lead almost every session. When the class was cancelled due to the Corona virus, we shifted to meeting by ZOOM calls on the dates and times originally scheduled for the class. It was estimated that we'd have round 10 students in the class, but once a couple of

---

[38] http://www.pachamama.org/about/origin-story
[39] See the Resources list at the end of this book for some videos of indigenous peoples sharing their stories.

Indigenous messages were shared, our enrollment exceeded 80 folks. As one of the attendees said after hearing Warm Springs artist and teacher Jefferson Greene share, "I've grown up around Indians and worked with them much of my life, and I learned more in an hour with Jefferson than I've ever known."

The sessions were recorded and, as part of this book's call to action, I'm working with a nonprofit organization, Pull Together Now, to create a library of the programs with links, categories, and brief descriptions, so that learners everywhere who are looking for authentic materials will have access to them. Our hope is that having such a 'library' will encourage other Earth-based stories to be told (and recorded) by those who've grown up with them—ancient stories, stories of wisdom transcending the pain brought by colonization, and stories of our return to living in harmony with Nature.

The Hopi model described above is an example of how such stories can help us understand the fundamental differences between Earth-based Indigenous cultures and empire-based Modernity cultures. They can help us choose which of the two exhibits the ethics on which we wish to build upon, as well as understand the processes that caused us to stray. The Hopi graphic presented above serves as a map of the territory and how to proceed. Now we must embody the territory, and we must do it quickly. But let's not rush, so we avoid taking shortcuts or making other bad decisions. We need time to change our assumptions, first.

### A Living Systems Point of View

Fortunately, the wisdom and understanding we are looking for is readily available in the sciences, if we just hold as a key principle that our Earth (and our Universe) is a living system. When the essence of living systems is understood, the ethics for being sustainable emerge. More, a way out of our current dilemma begins to become apparent. For example, in a debriefing session after a class, the teacher asked, "What is something from Theory of Knowledge that gave you hope?" A student stated that Natural

Systems Thinking was the most powerful. He described how, after reading the book *Ishmael*[40], which explains both how we got here and what's likely to occur, he felt discouraged, like we are all damned if we do and damned if we don't. This new way of thinking provided him a strategy to respond to the challenges of our world.

### Experiencing the Shift - Milt

A few years after retiring from IBM, a friend asked me to help him with a sustainability-oriented start-up company in which we were going to have to better understand the consciousness of all life. Once we had seed money and a prototype, I went back to graduate school at Antioch University in Seattle for a Masters degree in 'Whole System Design' in which the curriculum was primarily based on Living Systems. My graduation project was to see if I could get a small town in Oregon to define their desired future based on six facets of being sustainable, and in the process, persuade their public schools to develop the curricula necessary for both education in the schools and building a 'learning community.' My advisor, the late Dr. Elaine Jessen, insisted that I do a theory paper on my project. What became clear was that the theory that underlies sustainability of our continuously renewing Earth systems is Living Systems Theory.

Also, as part of my classwork, I was on a Design Team to teach Living Systems to my cohort, that was co-taught with Dr. Fritjof Capra. From that work I developed a Living Systems course that I now teach whenever I'm asked.

What follows is based on what I teach in the one period I'm generally allotted with the students. As far as I know, the material isn't part of any general curricula, and I believe it is an essential bridge for all of us who have been disconnected from Earth. The embodiment exercise I use in the class is the key to 'awakening an already knowing' in students, as well as both the paradigm shifts they wish to make in their lives and help facilitate in our culture.

---

[40] Daniel Quinn, *Ishmael: A Novel,* Bantam/Turner Books, 1992.

The sequence moves from the fundamental differences between a Mechanical and Living System; the attributes of all Living Systems; the gifts to which all life has been endowed; and ends with what I cal the Paradigm Shift Embodiment exercise.

## Mechanical & Living System Comparison

Most of us are well acquainted with mechanical systems: things like lawnmowers, cars, clocks, and washing machines. We recognize that they do what they're built to do, controlled by someone outside the system. There may be some variability in how they're used—for instance, when we go somewhere in our car, we take the route we choose, may or may not have passengers, and carry the belongings we'll need—but they do not evolve or choose.

| System Type | Mechanical | Living |
|---|---|---|
| **Structure** | Fixed | Self Organizing |
| **Organization** | Variable | Emergent |
| **Endowments** | None | Life Processes |
| **The whole is** | ≤ Sum of Parts | > Sum of Parts |
| **Science** | Newtonian | Quantum |
| **Attributes** | Constraints | Flourishing |

A living system is very different in many ways. It's structured to flourish, and is continually cleansing, healing and restructuring – evolving, if it and its environment are healthy, and *de*volving if it is not. But even if it devolves to death, it becomes a source of energy so that other life might flourish. As we observe the natural phenomena, we develop a systemic understanding of both what's going on both inside ourselves and all living systems, and how we are interdependent in this dance of life.

When preparing to teach Living Systems to the Antioch cohort, Fritjoff Capra shared the understanding that all life is endowed with certain life processes. I didn't understand what he meant at the time, but subsequent studies of the Ancient Hebrew language enlightened me regarding how Earth-based languages reflect these endowed processes.

## Education for Learning

From the understandings set forth so far this chapter, it becomes clearer that our public education system is failing us. The living-systems curricula is nowhere to be found in Science, Technology, Engineering and Math (STEM) Education.[41] More, when asked about this omission, educators respond with questions like:

→ Why should we teach that?

→ What should we replace in the current curricula?

→ What are the standards by which Living Systems should be measured?

Or they will state, "We already teach Biology, a Life Science." to which our response is, "but Biology is a reductionist science, focusing on pieces of the whole, and Living Systems are whole, with emergent properties."

This is all part of a much bigger problem in education: its basic philosophy.

Both of us have been students in the System Science PhD program at Portland State University, and Milt studied Peter Senge's, *The Fifth Discipline: The Art and Practice of the Learning Organization* as a text in his classes. He was strongly attracted to the notion of a *Learning Organization* and fortuitously met a manager from Intel, Bob Stensland, who worked with Dr. Senge on a regular basis to instill learning-organization processes in his work at Intel. Bob also worked with educators to bring Dr. Senge to Portland, along with three teachers who had implemented Senge's 5 Disciplines in a Middle School in Tucson, Arizona, to facilitate an in-service day and then have a meeting with local and state Department of Education (DOE) leaders.

Having become associated with that work, Milt was asked to attend a meeting on world-class education standards, where he asked, "What does a World-Class Education system look like?" The organizers responded, "We don't know." So Milt was asked head up a study to define an *Excellent Education System*.

---

[41] http://stemteachingtools.org/about

*Very difficult to introduce & integrate a relational way of thinking into a hierarchical system*

The study was structured around a clearly stated Vision, Purpose, and set of Principles, as well as three questions:

1) What was the intent with creating public education?
2) What were current best practices and how were they implemented? And
3) What is the education necessary to support the vision or Oregon's people?

The study was completed in less than 4 months and was well received at each checkpoint, until the last, where it was rejected. We were told it was because the Oregon Department of Education didn't know how to map this relational way of educating into their hierarchical system, and so the state went on to implement some very different comprehensive standards.

Ruth's experience was somewhat different. She graduated prior to Senge's publication so was using the principles without his processes in her work as a professor and director of a program that offered both undergraduate and graduate courses on systems and cybernetics in a state university. The program was cross-disciplinary, encouraging students from all majors to learn systems thinking and methods and apply them in their work. This created a problem within the university structure, which is defined by disciplines, or major fields of study, so the program was under constant scrutiny, having to defend its existence at every turn. The facts that students in our classes tended to do as well as or better than the majority of students in their major fields, and that our close relationship with companies around the university allowed us to develop a strong internship program that meant virtually all our graduates were hired before or soon after graduating, didn't make the situation easier, but seemed to enhance the university's concern about what we were doing and how.

The program lasted 17 years, underwent two internal evaluations and restructurings while Ruth was part of it, and built its curriculum around what it learned, some elements of which included:

→ The basic principles of systems are learned from experience and dialog more effectively than from texts;

→ The necessary experience can be created in a classroom setting or pulled from life and work;

→ Groups working together learn more effectively than individuals competing;

→ The process of becoming a team can be a means to learn to think systemically;

→ Maximal student learning occurs when the instructors' and students' understandings/ assumptions/models (sometimes called "paradigm") are clarified and written down at the beginning and end of a term of classes;

→ Computer modeling is a useful tool for clarifying thought processes and internal models/beliefs/assumptions (paradigm) about a focus of study;

→ Involving professionals who use the tools and methods of systems thinking in the learning process maximize both the students' and the faculty's effectiveness with those tools and methods.

The result was a dynamic program that expanded undergraduates' capacity to choose with intention and awareness of consequences while training graduate students to effectively facilitate working groups in every kind of work setting. The university administration, however, found too many conflicts with the traditional disciplinary field-of-study model and, in the name of budget management, ended up shutting down the program.

These lessons are relevant not just for our schools, but also business and governance institutions that are all structured hierarchically. If relational ways are introduced that then threaten the power-over assumptions of the hierarchy, they are shut down. In our culture the word 'leadership' connotes command and control, delegation, and alignment with top-down wisdom and instructions. This connotation has been supported by the myth that "Nature is red in tooth and claw," and its corollary myth: 'suvival of the fittest" meaning the strongest, when in fact, ecologists' recent research has established that Nature is primarily collaborative, not only to flourish individually, but collectively.

Schools are not alone in neglecting to design for emergence—they simply reflect the dominant values of the culture. Buildings in the U.S., for example, are built to last a decade, not a thousand years as they have in Europe, and the materials that were used to build them are tossed into a landfill when they are torn down and replaced.. The kind of limited thinking that we've described here is common throughout Modernity cultures, rooted in our hierarchical structures, linear alphabetic languages, and misplaced guiding principles. It is essential, therefore, that individual educators and alternative educational organizations help lead the shift so students are encouraged to seek their own best selves by awakening a knowing that has been obscured throughout most of their educational experience.

## Paradigms for Sustainable Living

The idea of different paradigms needed for sustainability was originally presented by Dr. Tom Gladwin, a Professor Emeritus of Sustainable Enterprise at the University of Michigan. He was the keynote speaker at a 'Systems Thinking for Sustainability' workshop in Portland in the mid-1990s, and after his speech, he gave us the quiz that he gave whenever he addressed an education or business group. The quiz had 20 questions designed to determine if our thinking was mechanical or organic, and 20 other interspersed questions discerning whether our worldview was primarily one of scarcity or abundance.

Dr. Gladwin concluded from his data that there are two basic archetypes:

→ 'Sustainability' folks who are very worried about 'Scarcity' caused by over-population, peak oil, peak soil, potable water, and clean air, and wish to deal with these shortages with compassion -- his connotation of 'Organic'.

→ 'Business' folks who believe 'Abundance' is infinite and they can take what they need and process it 'Mechanically.'

**Exploring & Expanding Archetypes – Milt**

 I had quite a bit of dissonance with his conclusions, primarily because I consider myself to be a sustainability person, but I don't think I reside in the upper-right hand quadrant. When I saw Dr. Gladwin the next day I asked him if he'd thought about the other two quadrants.

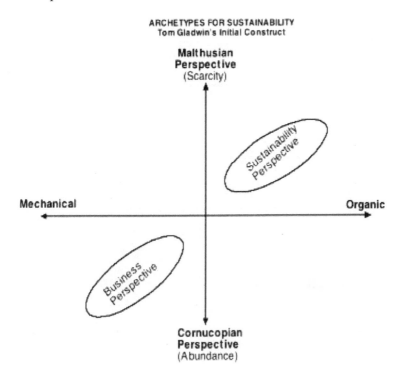

He said, 'No, what do you think they are?" I shared with him that I thought the upper-left hand quadrant was the 'Warring/Colonial' perspective: those who perceive scarcity and wish to bolster the realm of their power over. The lower-right quadrant I labeled the 'Indigenous', and I've now broadened it to be the 'Earth-based' perspective, seeking to include all peoples who recognize the importance of an ethic that honores Earth's processes.

ARCHETYPES FOR SUSTAINABILITY

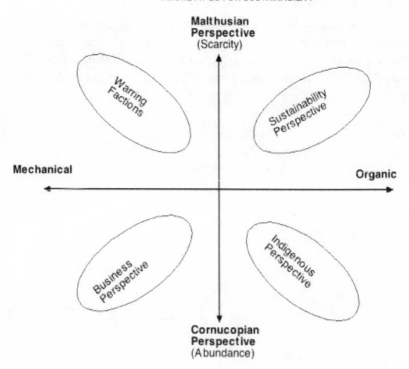

Malthusian
Perspective
(Scarcity)

Warring
Factions

Sustainability
Perspective

Mechanical                                                                        Organic

Business
Perspective

Indigenous
Perspective

Cornucopian
Perspective
(Abundance)

I knew I hadn't figured out how to properly name the upper right hand quadrant. It clearly didn't represent the 'Sustainability Perspective'. As I pondered the subject, attended other Sustainability workshops and conferences, and reflected on how all this fit together, I finally concluded that this quadrant was best labeled, 'Social Justice.'

I felt there was something very powerful about the axis Dr. Gladwin defined, but something fundamentally flawed with his conclusions. The problem lay in his quiz questions; they reflected his Western, Modernity culture's understanding of 'Organic' and 'Abundance'. With regard to the word 'Organic' Dr. Gladwin's questions assumed the Western Judeo-Christian ethic of 'Do not do unto others what you would not want done to yourself.' The Indigenous perspective is much broader: the Earth, perhaps the whole Universe, is alive, and has the following attributes:

→ All Earth's systems are alive and in continual flux as they cleanse, heal, and restructure -- always in emergent processes; and

→ All life has been endowed with several Life Processes, including perfect order (zero waste in Nature, organic life processes, natural laws of interdependence, possibility, energy, a life-death-life continuum, attraction) as well as love, awe, wonder, beauty, and wisdom;

→ All life has intrinsic value -- 'Domination' is a fabricated concept, a mistranslation of the Genesis story.

With regard to the word 'Abundance' the questions in the original quiz assumed that we can always take and take, whereas the Indigenous perspective is that Earth will always provide as long as we recognize the intrinsic value of all life, fulfill our mutual responsibilities, and honor the Covenant ov mutual support with our life-support dependencies. The Earth was given to us in an energetic balance and harmony, and if there's dissonance, we must clean it up so that we may live in gratitude and appreciation.

Now this is the comparison that I share with the students before they're asked to 'walk' the matrix.

I believe there are three required cultural paradigm shifts:

→ Shifting our thinking from *Mechanical* to *Organic – Systemic* as defined by the Earth-based cultures.

→ Shifting our world-view from *Scarcity* to *Abundance – Sufficient* as defined by the Earth-based cultures.

→ Shifting our action stance from the *Social Justice* to *Indigenous/Earth-based*.

As we apply these shifts we can see that the *Social Justice* issues of Modernity cultures largely dissolve with the adoption of a Living Systems perspective and the acceptance of Natural Law, Nature's example being relational–cooperative and essential for survival.

An Indigenous community responds with compassion to individuals who act outside the established norms, and protocols are established for restoring harmony with them and for inter-tribal relationships. In many of those cultures, any decision to go to war is controlled by elder women, the Clan Mothers, who make the final decision regarding entering a conflict, balancing the hot-headed, often hormone-driven, push for action by young warriors. The *Business* quadrant is not the same, either; when relational peoples operate around guiding principles that ensure both communal harmony and ecological integrity, rather than focusing mostly on returning dividends to shareholders. The emerging "B company" structure is a move in this direction, making it legal for a business to focus equally on "People, Planet, and Profit". But the community-building capitalism of Adam Smith's village-centric world is far more in line with this paradigm shift.

### The Shift Exercise

This exercise is done in a single class period and its original intent was to have the students recognize the three paradigm shifts we need to make as a culture. As importantly, it has served as an exercise in which many of the students embody a paradigm shift they wish to make in their own lives.

My preferred way of doing this exercise is to have the students in a circle with the following graphic on the floor in the middle. If the class is made up of youth or children and there are adults present, I ask the adults to serve as witnesses

Once I've determined that the students understand the matrix in terms of each quadrant, the meaning of each axis, and the information, I shared with them regarding the Earth-based perspective of 'Organic' as being systemic, and 'Abundance' as being sufficient.[42] I ask them to answer four (4) questions by walking to the quadrant that best answers each question for them.

→. Question 1: Which quadrant best describes who you're being at this stage in your life? And their response is overwhelmingly *Social Justice*.

---

[42] Note: The 3 quadrants labeled with 'K', are designated as such by Matthew Fox as Western 'Knowledge' cultures, and the Earth-based quadrant is labeled with a 'W' for Wisdom culture. When I discussed this with Seneca Elder Terry Cross, he said to me, "Milt, for me wisdom is knowledge that's understood relationally."

# ARCHETYPES FOR SUSTAINABILITY

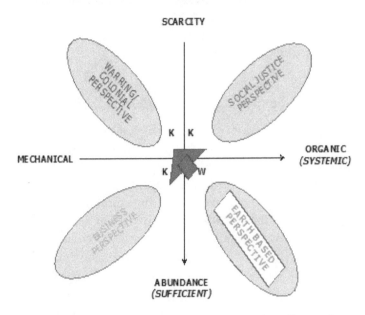

SCARCITY

WARRING/COLONIAL PERSPECTIVE

SOCIAL JUSTICE PERSPECTIVE

MECHANICAL

ORGANIC
(SYSTEMIC)

BUSINESS PERSPECTIVE

EARTH BASED PERSPECTIVE

ABUNDANCE
(SUFFICIENT)

→ Question 2: Which quadrant best describes who your parents' generation is being? Their response is again strong in terms of their movement to the *Business* quadrant.

→ Question 3: Which quadrant best describes who our government is being? Their response is once again strong, particularly when we're in bloody conflicts, to the *Warring/Colonial* quadrant.

→ Question 4: As you enter college or the work world, which is the quadrant that you wish to describe who you are being? Here there is an overwhelming response to be in the *Indigenous/Earth-based* quadrant.

Almost without exception, students exhibit a paradigm shift defined by their response to the 1st and 4th questions: the shift from the *Social Justice* to *Indigenous/Earth-based* quadrant. Mightn't it be reasonable that understanding Earth-based views of 'systemic' and 'sufficient' resonated with the students, perhaps awakened an already knowing? When I took the quiz over 25 years ago, since I understood the difference between 'systemic' and 'sufficient', I too had felt the dissonance of being placed in the *Social Justice* quadrant, and like the students, I knew that I belonged in the *Earth-based* quadrant.

## Living Systems in Our World

The realization that we can shift our understanding of the world from that of a mechanical clockwork to a living entity opens our minds and hearts to a whole new level of connection and understanding. We are no longer seeking to control a mindless structure whose activities are driven by random chance. Instead we're part of something that's alive; the life that is in us surrounds us, sustains us, and challenges us to find our place within it.

With that frame of reference, we approach everything from meal planning to construction to manufacturing with a very different set of criteria and intentions. We become mindful of our relation to and interactions with the rest of the world. And we begin to find new ways to do things.

### Living Applications - Ruth

In my work, whether it was helping to rebuild derelict houses in an inner city, running a college program, raising a family, or helping a church to grow, the realization that I was working with a living entity with multiple sets of interactions and potentials that were working together to thrive as a whole, has informed every accomplishment.

I remember the first time I realized that a lake was a living system. Suddenly, it wasn't just a basin of rocks filled with water that someone had dumped some fish into; I could see and feel how it was an intricately balanced set of relationships between rocks, water, soil, and various plants, fish, insects, amphibeans, and micro-organisms—all working together with the sun to facilitate the clarity of the water and the well-being of all the creatures living in it. Later, when my children were young, they sometimes visited my classroom and I would introduce them as a system, inviting the students to explain how and why. Then I'd ask how and why the room full of students was a system.

This perspective led to a series of classes—and a book, called *Home*—suggesting what a new culture, based on a living-systems perspective, along with ancient methods and our current science and technology, might look like.[43] In that book I suggested that we work from the following principles:

→ Each person, household, and community is a living system

→ Living systems can be essentially self-sufficient in an environment containing their essential requirements.

→ The methods of permaculture, relying on and mimicking natural processes, make self-sufficiency a low-toil, easy-maintenance process.

→ A river basin or watershed contains all the resources required for human systems to thrive.

→ Maximizing the availability of essential resources is possible only when all aspects and activities within the river basin/watershed and the human systems are understood and appreciated.

→ Individuals and communities that share, appreciate each other, and work cooperatively accomplish more over longer periods than when they compete.

→ Creating opportunities for children to understand, appreciate, share, and cooperate with other kinds of living systems leads to long-term, sustainable communities.

These principles have been demonstrated, not only in biological and ecological systems, but also in the human systems we've been calling Indigenous or Earth-based cultures, and they have stood the test of time.

---

[43] *Home: Creating Humanity's Future* by Ruth L. Miller, Portal Center Press, 2018.

## Systemic Understanding

*The greatest revolution of our time is in the way we see the world. The mechanistic paradigm underlying the Industrial Growth Society gives way to the realization that we belong to a living, self-organizing cosmos....*
*This realization changes everything. It changes our perceptions of who we are and what we need, and how we can trustfully act together for a decent, noble future.*

*~ Joanna Macy*[44]

The graphic below describes a process that is very prevalent in modern cultures, where perhaps millions of well meaning people and thousands of organizations are dedicated to making our world more sustainable, and their work is labeled *Holding Actions* because they're not significantly contributing to a *Paradigm Shift.*

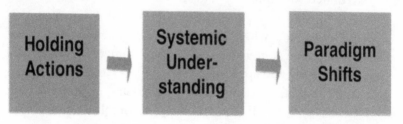

Chart is adapted from Joanna Macy's work

An example of such holding actions might be all the people and organizations dedicated to addressing one facet or another of our Climate Crisis, but climate change has barely been affected.

*Systemic Understanding* in this case is recognizing how a human action affects a natural state that in turn affects other life support systems. An example is the Tar Sands project in the Northwest Territories of Canada where massive, invasive extractions have caused, among other things, pollution of rivers that flow to the oceans where it adversely affects oceanic plant life on which the fish feed, their ability to procreate, and eventually limits the fish as

---

[44] https://www.joannamacy.net/

a food source. We begin to discern how we live downstream from virtually every action, including our own.

This is just one of several disastrous effects from the Tar Sands project. There is also massive deforestation, poisoning of local fish, humans with cancers that far exceed previous experience, diminished animal life procreation, and more, each of which has its own systemic implications. Often times the affects compound, rather than being linear, and thus we begin to understand the exponential nature of change and how tipping points are created.

It should be noted that *Systemic Understanding* includes humans as part of Nature; thus Modernity culture's separation from Nature obscures our understanding of how things really work. More, *Systemic Understanding* is embedded in the wisdom of the ancient, Earth-based languages, as we explored in the chapter on *Living Languages.*.

## Spiral Dynamics

The embodiment exercise described in the previous chapter maps very well and lends insights into the *Spiral Dynamic* model[45] developed by Beck and Cowan in 1995, that will help clarify an approach for accepting the Earth-based ethic as a culture, once again. Their model, as shown on the next page, describes how every culture starts at the Beige meme, or level of understanding itself and the world, and progresses through each of the other memes until its members aren't capable of progressing any further.

Looking at the chart on the next page, we can see that some cultures flowed smoothly to the Turquois meme, while others, like our own, got attracted to the power and control of hierarchy. If it is severe, they regress back to the Red meme, and if isn't severe they end up in the Blue, Orange, and Green memes.

---

[45] *Spiral Dynamics: Mastering Values, Leadership and Change* Don Edward Beck & Christopher C. Cowan, Wiley, 1995

When a few cultures disconnected from the Earth-based understandings thousands of years ago, their ability to think systemically (Yellow) was greatly diminished, and they could no longer flow through to the Turquoise meme, where they could function in their highest capacities..

So, while empire-bassed Modernity cultures generally believe that they represent the most advanced, civilized ways of being, this is not the case. As the students in the exercise described in the previous section showed us when they expressed how they're being in their lives today by moving to the *Social Justice* quadrant, they were acting in the Green meme—the highest meme generally exhibited in Modernity cultures.

**Turquoise – Spiritual & Highly Evolved**

**Yellow – Systemic Understanding**

**Green -- Social Justice**

**Orange – Benevolent Hierarchy**

**Blue – Hierarchically Controlling**

**Red -- Power Over**

**Purple – Clans & Placate Spirits**

**Beige – Basic Needs for Survival**

And when they chose the Earth-based meme for who they wish to be in their adult lives, something had been awakened in them. They had absorbed enough *Systemic Understanding* of life processes to move through the Yellow meme to the Turquoise.Then, when the students placed their parents' generation in the *Business* quadrant of Milt's graph, their parents could have been acting in the Blue or Orange meme, and when they judged the country to be *Warring Colonizers,* they were placing us nationally in the Red meme. Thus the students showed us hallmarks of our culture—dominated by power-over (Red), and reacting to it with social justice needs (Green).

It should be clear now that the root cause of the Ethical dilemma discussed in the Introduction not only began with people's separation from the Earth several thousand years ago, it has been significantly compounded by cultures succumbing to the attraction of power-over. This break has not only inhibited cultures from moving up to the highest memes but has pulled cultures down from those memes. The Spiral Dynamic model thereby helps us understand how we've institutionalized and maintained not working in harmony with natural processes and therefore being sustainable.

## Bringing Life to the Matrix

With these understandings it seems to us that it is therefore essential to include Living Systems curricula in all our education endeavors, and borders on criminal that such ideas are not included in the U.S. national Science, Technology, Engineering and Math ((STEM[46]) Programs.

What if we could discern all our fields of study, each conversation, and all of the people and organizations with whom we interact, as alive and synergistically connected? What if we saw the world in terms of dynamic interactions?

A starting point might be to take the 2x2 matrix used for the student's embodiment exercise described above and add to it the factors that encourage folks to flow from one quadrant to another. Then we could apply artistic creativity as in drama, music, dance, poetry, animation and audience participation, to bring life to those flows. Such a model could help us approach resolving our current ethical dilemma and its consequences—based in part on a new understanding of what we've wrought—and is illustrated on the next page.

---

[46] http://stemteachingtools.org/about

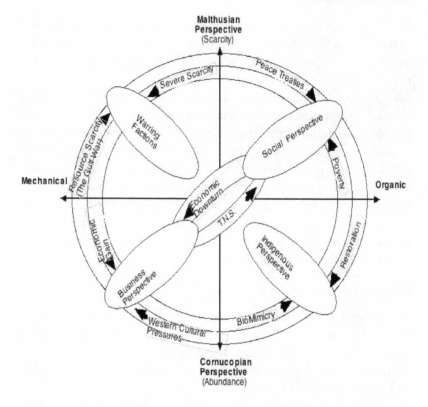

The Malthusian Perspective (Scarcity), Mechanical, Organic, and Cornucopian Perspective (Abundance) axes with perspectives including Severe Scarcity, Peace Treaties, Warring Factions, Social Perspective, Poverty, Resource Scarcity (The Gulf War), Economic Downturn, T.N.S., Economic Gain, Restoration, Business Perspective, Indigenous Perspective, Western Cultural Pressures, and BioMimicry.

## The Concept of Chaord

Modernity culture often describes Nature as chaotic, but both modern science and ancient wisdom tell us it is not. And this new way of thinking has been articulated by Dee Hock in his book, *Birth of the Chaordic Age*, where he explains that there is a little-known organizing principle that underlies natural processes, and will need to be understood and applied in designing for emergence. It's based on the paradox of blending order and chaos.

Hock coined the term 'chaord' to describe systems that may be perceived as chaotic at one level, but are actually ordered when discerned from a different perspective. Hock described 'chaordic' as

*the behavior of a self-governing organism or system that harmoniously blends what were previously conceived to be opposites, such as chaos and order, or cooperation and competition.*[47]

Specifically, chaord is defined as:

1. The behavior of any self-governing organism, organization or system which harmoniously blends characteristics of order and chaos.
2. Patterned in a way dominated by neither chaos nor order.
3. Characteristic of the fundamental organizing principles of evolution and nature.

Hock writes that chaordic systems have the following attributes:

→ An elegantly simple structure
→ Clear purpose
→ Grounded in guiding principles
→ Blending of apparent opposites

As demonstrated by the students in the exercise described above, one of our three necessary paradigm shifts is to change our perspective on the world from Mechanical to Organic, and that includes changing our primary scientific assumptions from those of Newtonian physics to Living Systems dynamics. With the recognition that all natural and human processes are those of living systems, we can begin to look at, not only our environments, but all our organizations, institutions, conversations, and projects, as alive. We can discern much more clearly how to intervene with organizational problems when we ask what brings life to, and takes life from the system we're observing, and when we map organizational behaviors onto the Panarchy cycle. We can be more effective by designing, not for control, but for emergence—after all, isn't this what learning and development is all about?

---

[35]Dee Hock, 'What is Enlightenment' Interview,
http://www.wie.org/j22hockintro.asp

## For Reflection

The building of bridges that help us understand how other cultures know what we don't know but resonates deeply within is just beginning. Consider the following –

> ➤ What are the other bridges that need to be developed, and how should they be taught?
>
> ➤ Do some cultures exhibit a fundamentaly different intelligence than our culture?
>
> ➤ What can only be truly learned if it is taught by those who have experienced it?
>
> ➤ How can we accept that when we get a glimpse of a knowing that we must listen and learn to uncover what underlies that knowing?
>
> ➤ What might we offer the Earth Based Peoples in exchange for their already knowing – perhaps we need to ask them what they'd like from us?

# 6. Toward A Culture of Connection

## Discovering & Learning

The possibilities before us are endless, but, as with all panarchic systems, they are becoming more and more chaotic every day that we remain attached to old structures and ideas. Today, with empire-based Modernity culture controlling the activities of most of the population, humanity has a choice: remain attached to the ethics and actions of the dominant culture, or allow a new seed, a new ethic, a new set of possibilities, based on living languages from ancient cultures, to begin to take root.

Such a choice requires the kind of examination we've been describing thus far in this book. But there's more. In order to actually experience the possibilities inherent in the new seed-culture, we need to turn our minds away from the familiar past and toward a radically different framework for understanding and action—we need a real paradigm shift, a transformation of consciousness.

### Transformative Learning Experience – Milt

Let me share with you an example of a transformative learning experience for me. I was taking a class titled, *"Business as a Living System"* taught by Dr. Tom Johnson of the Portland State University (PSU) Business School. Part of our reading was the manuscript for a book he was co-authoring titled, *Profit Beyond Measure: Extraordinary Results Through Attention*. In the book he tells a story of the CEO from Ford visiting a Japanese plant in the early 1980's, when Ford was in serious financial straits. The CEO had never seen a manufacturing operation like Toyota's and asked his host the source of Toyota's uniqueness. The embarrassed host told him, "The River Rouge Ford plant in Michigan."

This was surprising because the Ford CEO was accustomed to seeing was a very segmented workstation environment in which components from the car were all built *en masse*, assembled at the end of the manufacturing process, and after a quality check, often sent back for rework. What he saw in Japan instead was a manufacturing flow in which each worker knew what was expected from the person who passed work to him or her, and the quality required of the part or assembly that he or she was passing to the next worker. It turned out that if there was a problem, each person was authorized to shut down the production line, and all were expected, without blame, to participate in solving the problem in a way that met quality objectives and had minimum impact on the process. There was a natural rhythm to the work, and it is often said by those who consult and help develop these kinds of processes that they know it is working when they can "hear the music."

I tell this story because the standard American Ford process was developed by what we perceive to be our smartest engineers. As such, the process is a product of our mechanical way of thinking—based in reductionism—in which the worker is limited in knowledge about the process and does just one task to the specifications created by someone else, with an underlying assumption that workers need to do just what they're told. Toyota's process, on the other hand, is an organic flow, and assumes that a well-informed work force has a quality ethic and will add value to the manufacturing process as well as contribute to customer satisfaction. At that time only a handful of Americans could discern the Japanese approach to manufacturing as more effective and efficient in the long run. We were, as a culture, myopic.

This is the nature of cultural paradigm shifts. We had to learn to "suspend disbelief", to be open to learning from others, and in most cases make a shift in our worldview from mechanical to organic – discerning life as a living system and appreciating other cultures and Nature as mentors and models.

This was a significant learning for me that was made much easier because of my own work experiences with Japanese manufacturing plants while I was with IBM. One such experience came in the late 1970's, when IBM was delaying its announcement of the new S/370 computer, the heart and soul of its product line.

The reason for the delay was our inability to produce satisfactory yields of logic modules using newly developed microchip technology. We had tried in the U.S. and Germany without success, and so we turned to the Japanese. I was privileged to be on the team from the U.S. headquarters of IBM that evaluated the Japanese plan, and it was through this process that I began to understand their guiding principles: continuous flow, a quality ethic embedded in everyone, and the futility of both rework and hierarchical evaluation processes. The Japanese produced the S/370 modules with yields that were higher, at a cost that was lower, than originally specified. I think it's fair to say that each of us on the headquarters team had our understanding of best practices in manufacturing transformed.

As a footnote to this story, one of the best presentations I ever saw was the Japanese explaining to the Americans that in order to be successful, we couldn't impose any more of our values on them—this had to be done the Japanese way.

## *Building Community*

### Appreciative Inquiry – Milt

In May of 2002 our visiting professor at Antioch Seattle was Dr. David Cooperrider, the developer of Appreciative Inquiry (A-I).[48] He shared with us a story of how, during his Ph.D. studies, he asked employees of a medical clinic in Cleveland a very neutral question regarding their work. He reported that 90% or more answered in terms of a problem with which they were dealing, while less than 10% told of how they were doing their life work and the fulfillment they received. David's thesis built on the insight that experience gave him and was the beginning of A-I, an authentic process for surfacing virtues while acknowledging problems, and coming to action in ways that do what needs doing

---

[48] developed at Case Western Reserve University's department of organizational behavior, starting with a 1987 article by David Cooperrider and Suresh Srivastva: https://en.wikipedia.org/wiki/Appreciative_inquiry

in a manner consistent with one's principles. I was so taken with the method that I became a certified facilitator: gratitude for all life is at the heart of this book, and Appreciative Inquiry has proven to be an incredible tool for developing this appreciative way of being.

The project that met the final requirement for my graduation from the Whole System Design program at Antioch University stemmed from a conversation I'd had with our State School Superintendent regarding an Executive Order by our Governor to achieve a sustainable State by 2025. My question to her was: "How do our sustainability efforts in Oregon inform public education and what role will our public schools play in achieving our State goal?" Based on that conversation, I set out to find a small community and its school system to work together to define both a sustainable future and the learning that would need to take place both in the school and the community. Through a colleague, Dr. Ed Smith, in the Reynold's School District just east of Portland, I found a school with the ideal principal, Patricia Martinez. My initial work was to cement relationships with Patricia and the city planners in Fairview, Oregon where her school is located.

I used the A-I process extensively, and successfully, to enroll faculty, parents, and a Steering Committee at Fairview. Our project, 'Imagine Fairview' was to a degree modeled after a similar project, "Imagine Chicago.' Our plan had three phases:

1. Convene a Community meeting to hear of the city's vision and articulate it from a sustainable perspective.
2. Work with the educators to develop curricula and instruction for both the school and the city.
3. Set up an ongoing education and implementation program.

Phase 1 of the project was a very big success. In order to get the faculty to buy into the project, I asked Patricia if I could have half an hour of her next staff meeting to get their commitment. She obliged, and when I met with the faculty, I asked them for their cooperation in discovering what brings life to their jobs. In the process I used a very simple Appreciative Inquiry that asked each teacher to get in touch with a deeply moving moment in their own learning, one that was an incredible 'aha,' and that both influenced them to be teachers and continues to influence how they teach today. They paired up and were allotted three minutes to share their experiences. The energy was palpable, and once quieted, we talked about the experience of sharing their stories. Two points were made that I'll probably never forget. First, a young man said, "I didn't understand what you meant when you said, 'What brings life to my job,' and now I know." And then a group of teachers converged on the notion that they wanted appreciation to be a virtue in their culture.

I think a little of the joy of this process was recognizing that everyone in the room had such a story, they were delighted to tell it, and even more delighted that there was deep listening for what they had to say. The storytelling experience created a strong bond within each pair, and the later sharing connected everyone. I then explained the project I was proposing and asked for their support, and I'm happy to say they responded in the affirmative.

Through this process I confirmed a strong intuitive feeling that it makes far more sense to experience A-I then to try to learn about it through reading or a presentation. The same experiential approach was used when I met with PTA members, the planning team we pulled together, and many of the city folks from Fairview. Almost every Fairview citizen with whom I met told me that my Community Meeting would never work. They told me of the social rifts within their community: old timers vs. recent arrivals, geographical disputes, and social status differences. I told each of them that I trusted the process, and that I believed the A-I bonding would mitigate their simmering differences. I'm very happy to say that I was correct, because I have doubts about my own facilitation skills when there is conflict. Where other facilitators might focus on conflict resolution, I've found that A-I is a terrific tool for minimizing, and often avoiding, conflict. I was feeling more and more like I could overcome the 'impossible.'

The graphic on the next page is the Appreciative Inquiry schematic that I used to design the Community Day. The

'Definition' phase is one I added to the normal 4-phase cycle, to include our invitation process described above.

**THE APPRECIATIVE INQUIRY CYCLE**

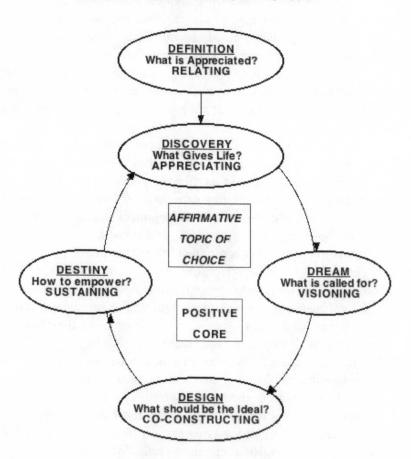

The 'Discovery', 'Dream', 'Design', and 'Destiny' phases of the A-I process always revolve around a well-defined 'Affirmative Topic of Choice' and a set of guiding principles and agreed upon virtues named the 'Positive Core'.

One of the most wonderful uses of A-I was for inviting people to our Community Meeting. Our tact was to have students do inter-generational interviews, and we developed age-appropriate Appreciative Inquiries with the following theme:

*Please think of someone who you very much appreciate and perhaps you haven't either thanked them or told them the depth of your gratitude. Please call this person, thank them and request an interview. The primary question is: "What inspired you to perform the act of kindness?" Listen attentively to what they have to say and take only enough notes so that you'll remember the gist of their story; thank them for their time and for their kindness and invite them to our Community Meeting.*

The smaller children usually picked a parent or a teacher, and the feedback was always positive and very sweet.

I worked with a high school economics class whose students came back with the most incredible stories, many of which brought tears to our eyes. One pretty big, tough young man's experience was of someone who had brought him a glass of water on a very hot day when he was doing yard work. When he asked his benefactor what inspired this act of kindness, he was told that when he was young he used to always fight with his brothers. One day, quite suddenly, their father passed away, and the brothers realized how important they were to each other. He said that the brothers never fought again, and he had become a kinder person. It struck me that this and other stories, in addition to being very powerful, had an organic feel. They often didn't have the linear cause and effect that I'd grown to expect in stories.

When we finished hearing each student, the teacher, Ms. Jennifer Faro, was obviously deeply touched, and she shared two points with the class. First, she asked if anyone could relate what we'd just done with the economic theories and equations they'd been learning. None of them could. She explained that the theories and equations they were learning would be necessary to know when they entered the workforce, and of course they needed to know them to pass her tests. But, more importantly, if they were to advance in their work and solve more complex problems, it was the appreciation of people and relationship building that was at the heart of a strong, effective organization.

Her second comment was that this class would never be the same, that what they had shared and the appreciation they had for each other would positively affect their learning together.

We had completed the 'Definition' phase of A-I with our invitation process and in the process set the theme and tone for our day-long Community Meeting.

When that meeting actually happened, almost 80 townspeople participated and were genuinely excited to both share their stories and focus on the future of their community. The agenda for the Community meeting followed the A-I Cycle as it flows from phase to phase, and key understandings regarding the 'Affirmative Topic of Choice' and 'Positive Core' served as our design points for the day. After a welcome from the school principal, Patricia Martinez, we began our communal work with the step called 'Discovery', intended to put people in touch with their caring for the Fairview Community and their sense of place. When that was completed, I told them about the A-I Process and how it would be central for the rest of our work that day. We discussed the 'Affirmative Topic of Choice' and 'Creating Fairview as a Sustainable Community', and we reviewed four Key Principles that were our 'Positive Core:'

1) People and organizations aren't problems but sources of Wisdom;
2) Avoidance of all Deficit Language;
3) Inclusion of all stakeholders in a Relational Environment; and
4) Reconnection with our 'Latent' Virtues.

We added the virtues from our 'Discovery' process to the Key Principles, and agreed upon our 'Positive Core'. I then reviewed our agenda for the day that consisted of the following segments:

→ The Fairview town planners presented a document called 'Fairview Vision 2022' as the basis for our dreaming;
→ We presented six facets of their vision in terms of sustainability attributes:
   o Protecting Natural Resources,
   o Sustainable Industries,

   o  Renewable Energy,
   o  Public Recreation,
   o  Revitalizing Downtown, and
   o  Strengthening Community

→ Participants selected two facilitated conversation topics; one from the first three sustainability attributes, and one from the last three.

→ Following these conversations everyone met to share what the participants had developed, from which we had the framework for the 'Design" phase.

→ We closed with an appreciative reflection and sharing process intended to give everyone a new sense of what our 'Destiny' might be.

Unfortunately, the project was terminated shortly after the Community Meeting. First, the city determined that they didn't have the money or staff to continue their support. I had made a tactical error by finding a school first and then going to the city planners where the school was located. I now believe that each city or town must self-select so that they are motivated, and there should be a qualification process to be sure that they are committed and ready to move forth. Second, the teachers said that they were required to remain too focused on achieving Oregon's standards- oriented programs to develop new curricula on their own. With the help of a colleague I approached the State and was told that legislative and financial issues were in the way.

I now believe that we were just a little ahead of our time, and as municipalities become more focused on sustainability, and schools come to terms with how our sustainability efforts inform public education, and visa versa, we may be able dust off the project, revise it, and have a model for seeding and nurturing sustainability at the heart of each community—through the schools. In fact, fourteen years later, as I drove through Fairview with Ilarion Merculieff and told him this story, and he said, "You need to resurrect the project." My plan is to do just that as part of the ongoing process of *Awakening an Already Knowing*, and now I'll suggest that we use the *100% Consensus* Interview process (described below) to get all the contributing parties on board before we start, as well as relationship-building and effective implementation processes if there are contentious feelings.

I continue to use A-I as a relationship-building tool whenever I design or facilitate a gathering, and I find that people are transformed when they connect with their most cherished virtues and they love to tell their stories. Often individuals after experiencing sharing an intimate story with someone they've never met before will say something to the effect, "I feel as if I've just met a soul-mate." And often a whole community will be transformed by the experience of sharing and following that with 'Dreaming', Designing', then feeling a new sense of 'Destiny', defined as "the inner purpose of a life that can be discovered and realized."

With a tool like Appreciative Inquiry it bcomess clear that overcoming the impossible is often just a state of mind..

### Transforming a Membership Organization with A-I – Ruth

Milt introduced me to A-I some years ago and I, too, have found it useful in a number of settings. The most profound effect I've witnessed was when I used the process to facilitate an organization through their first all-member vision-creating event. Previous to this event the board had set the vision, plans, and budget for the organization and then persuaded volunteers to implement what the board had decided. It had worked, sort of. The organization had continued for 20 years with a couple dozen folks and had their own meeting-space.

I was brought in when one member of the board saw the possibility of including more people and having a larger impact in the community—which seemed to need what this group was doing. After some months of participating in the organization's events and encouraging a few changes in their process, I suggested that it was time to learn what the membership wanted the organization to be and to design the next year's budget around that. The board considered the idea for a few meetings and finally agreed to an all-day member meeting that I would facilitate.

We then let the members know what we had planned and asked people to reserve a spot. About ½ of the members, and a few "friends" who participated but had not yet joined, said they would attend. In the end, about ¾ of the regular attendees participated in the event.

We held the meeting "off-site", that is, we went to a different meeting space and arranged for all who attended to have drinks, snacks, and a meal during the day. Boardmembers did all the set-up and support, and the board president opened and closed the day. We had chart paper and easels in various places around the room for a visible record of what the membership had to say, and used large-tip markers so people could see the words clearly.

I explained the essential process described by Milt, above, and then asked a question: "What do we love about this organization?" The answers came slowly at first, but soon built up speed to the point where other folks came up to help write down what was being said. The mood in the room increased to joyful excitement as people shared their happy stories and experiences and the qualities of the organization those demonstrated. After about 20 minutes, I recapped what had been written and asked if we'd missed anything. A few more words were added to the lists, and then we posted the lists on the wall in the front of the room as a reference point for the rest of the day. This was the "Discovery" part of the process.

I then asked, "Given that we love these things, what do we want to see more of?" Now that they were comfortable that they would be heard and recorded without comment or criticism, people didn't hesitate to offer their suggestions. Again, volunteer recorders came up to write the responses down. And again, the energy increased as people thought about what it would be like to have even more of the qualities they appreciated about this organization, about what would bring them more fully into it, and what might encourage others to participate. Every now and then someone would voice a concern or a criticism, which I would then turn around and offer as a positive statement of what they would like to see more of—in the form of a question. For example, a participant might say: "we don't have enough space in the kitchen." To which I would say something like: "Sounds like you appreciate having a kitchen and would like more space in it; is that correct?" Almost always, they would agree and we'd write "more kitchen space" or whatever the issue was, and that was sufficient to keep the flow of ideas going.

Again, after about 20 minutes, I re-capped what was on the sheets and asked if there was anything we'd missed. And again, a few people would add something, or occasionally would notice that something had not been recorded. When they were done we had the "Dream".

A lunch break followed. I used the time to group the ideas into categories: physical space, administration, programs, education, community outreach and service, etc.

When we reconvened I showed the group the categories and invited them to choose which category they would like to spend more time working on. They broke into groups, and, using the sheets from the morning, began to identify specific actions and activities that would bring about the "more of" that had been listed for that category. If no one chose to work on a category, that was fine; it simply meant we weren't ready as an organization to build that "Dream," or to take that "More" on.

For about half an hour the groups brainstormed (using brainstorming rules: everything counts; no judgement, criticism, or "we've tried that"; everyone gets heard) and explored possible actions through which the organization could have more of what they loved. The groups ranged from 3-7 people, seated around tables with large sheets of chart paper and big-tipped markers, so what they came up with could be seen by the whole room when they were done. Everyone present was engaged and excited. The board president and I moved around the room, available to answer questions as needed.

After a quick break, the whole membership reconvened to hear what the groups had come up with. With each presentation the energy in the room increased, as the members began to see ways they could have more of what they loved actually happen.

When the presentations were complete, their charts were posted on the wall (actually windows, at this point—we'd used up the wall space with the "Discovery" and "Dream" charts!). The next phase was commitment. Each person in the room was asked to sign their name on a chart next to one or more of the actions that the groups had come up with to make their dreams for the organization come true. This was their commitment to show up and participate in that activity, to help make it happen.

Amazingly, everyone in the room signed up for at least one action, which is phenomenal, as it would all be done as volunteers. Again, the energy was high, as people chose to do what they most enjoyed, what they were good at, or something they wanted to learn about, knowing this was just a year-long commitment and could be renegotiated at any time.

Another short break followed, during which the board-members and I collated the information and encouraged folks to write down what they'd committed to do.

The board president closed the meeting with a summary of what the group had committed to, laying out the "Destiny" of the organization for the next year. He congratulated the membership on a powerful visioning session generating what looked to be a very powerful action-plan for the year ahead. I committed to typing up the information on the charts, which would be included in the next newsletter.

And, over the next year, over ¾ of the actions laid out in that session were implemented, the organization grew by 50%, and doubled its outreach services in the community. More people began to attend programs and participate in various activities, as well. Needless to say, the process was repeated the next year— with twice as many participants and very similar results.

## Honoring Ways of Knowing

Because everyone comes from different backgrounds and have different genetic structures, every person is unique in how they listen, what they hear, how they take in information, how they process what they take in, how they store that information, and how they communicate what they remember. Part of the power of processes like Appreciative Inquiry and Brainstorming is that they allow the freedom for individuals to take in, process, and share in their own unique way.

## The Human Dynamics Model

The best work we knew of to explain the differences between how the Western 'Knowledge' cultrs and Earth-based 'Wisdom' cultures learn and process information is the model called Human Dynamics by Dr. Sandra Seagal and her colleagues.[49]

Dr. Seagal developed her understanding by following her own "Already Knowing" that people's voices resonated for her in different parts of her body--some in her chest, others around her mouth, and still others higher in her head. She would invite small groups who resonated in one area or the other to her home to cook a meal together, and after they'd eaten, share what was important to them in conversation. What she found was that the groups representing each area were distinctly different, and that diverse groups who resonated within her in the same area were very similar in certain respects. Seagal concluded that human beings are born with one of three preferences (Physical, Emotional, or Mental) for how we take in information and another one of three preferences (also labeled Physical, Emotional, or Mental) for how we process it.

She labeled these preferences "Dynamics" and in her model, there are nine possible Human Dynamics emanating from a 3x3 construct (illustrated on the next page).

As she went around the world teaching her theory and helping people identify their own dynamic, she collected data from the people she met and worked with. The data shows that the percentages of the dynamics from one culture to another vary widely. In Western cultures about 85% of the population process emotionally: 1/3 of these are Emotional about their ideas, and the other 2/3 are Emotional about their immediate feelings. On the other hand, people from Indigenous and many Eastern cultures have a very high percentage that process physically. And, where

---

[49] Sandra Seagal and David Horne, *Human Dynamics: A Foundation for the Learning Organization*, 1994.

Western cultures tend to be oriented on the individual, Indigenous peoples tend to focus on the group.

**Taking In Information**

|  | Physical | Mental | Emotional |
|---|---|---|---|
| **Emotional** |  |  |  |
| **Mental** |  |  |  |
| **Physical** |  |  |  |

*(left axis: Processing Information)*

Few people are surprised by these differences, yet people in our culture don't try to explain them, and some mistakenly conclude that some ways of processing are inherently better than others. The fact is that each dynamic has its strengths and weaknesses, and we all need to appreciate each type of processing and learn how to integrate them internally as individuals and collectively in groups.

To demonstrate this, Sandra Seagal and her husband, David Horne, selected triads of young students by their sets of dynamics and videotaped them as they built model playgrounds. The differences among dynamics are clear in how the students reacted to each other, related to the materials, what they produced, and how they viewed their work. One professor who saw the video commented, "I've just seen five beautiful works of art (the models), none of which I could assess accurately if I didn't know the student's dynamic, and none of which I could judge fairly if I didn't know my own dynamic."

## Human Dynamics and Cultural Differences

The predominant dynamic in Indigenous cultures is Physical-Emotional, that is, they bring in information to which they are deeply connected (Emotional) and process it systemically (Physical). By contrast, the Western schools' predominant processing is Emotional, with the preponderance of teachers' culture being Physical-Emotional and the administrative culture being Mental-Emotional. Information for the former is based on feelings and for the latter on the intellect. The Human Dynamics website describes the problems that arise as a result:

> *In schools in the United States, Canada, Sweden, and Israel where we've worked, we've found 50 to 60 percent of the children identified as having learning problems to be physical-emotional, though they represent only 5 to 10 percent of the population. Often, they're labeled "slow learners." To date, we've found few of these children to be actually learning disabled.*[50]

It's readily accepted by most people that Indigenous and Eastern cultures think more holistically in that they're more inclusive, consider generational consequences, and have an intuitive understanding of being in harmony with the Earth. Yet, clearly, the Western Modernity culture approach to teaching and learning does not work for them.

Among educators, there's an acceptance that our schools don't seem to understand where learning begins for most Indigenous students, which lack the Human Dynamics model addresses the problem effectively. Generally speaking, physical-emotional individuals need two crucial elements: physical involvement in the learning process, and time for individual exploration, absorption, and digestion.

To help the physical-emotional learner, educators need to present extremely clear instructions, preferably presented as a series of steps. These learners must understand the practical

---

[50] http://www.humandynamicsfoundation.com/humandynamicsreading.html

purpose and utility of the material and how they will be expected to use it before they can really absorb it.

As we consider the amount of learning that is necessary to address our current global crises, our challenge is clear when we recognize that virtually no one knows either their own dynamic or the dynamic of others for taking in and processing information. The following questions and responses arise:

→ In addition to the mental and emotional intelligences that are so widely recognized in western Modernity culture, might there also be a physical intelligence?

o   The answer is quite clearly 'yes' and is exhibited wherever there is mutuality with Nature and all life forms.

→ Why isn't this model widely used within and across cultures?

o   Quite probably because the colonized cultures don't trust the colonizers to accept that each dynamic is equal in that it brings unique valued, necessary perspectives to bear.

→ Might Human Dynamics be accepted as a useful tool in Indigenous Pedagogy?

o   Quite probably 'yes' because indigenous peoples tend to be more inclusive and holistic, and will understand that all perspectives are necessary for addressing concerns.

We recognize that this is by no means the only model of human behavior and learning tendencies available. What is clear to us, however, is that this one helps to clarify the distinctions between people raised in the western, empire-based, Modernity cultures and those who were not. It also shows us what areas those who were raised the western cultures need to develop in order to more fully embody the wisdom of Earth-based, Indigenous people.

Dr. Jean Pence, principle of the Merlo Station Community School (described later in this book) and Milt are both well-versed in Human Dynamics. They co-facilitated a workshop to help a middle-school staff understand Five Disciplines described in Peter Senge's book *The Fifth Discipline* and found that there was virtually no understanding of systems thinking. They decided to take a problem the school staff were all familiar with, dealing with a delinquent student, and talk about it from five Human Dynamic perspectives, as a way to introduce the idea of systems thinking. The teachers and administrators were asked, "When you think of the student and the trouble he's in as a system, which of the following system stories resonates most deeply with you?"

1.  The immediate family, school, court, and friends and how they might feel, support or turn on the student. What more could you have done? Will the student be OK?

2.  A problem that is more clearly seen as a set of activities—a project with objectives that needs to be sequenced with milestones and measurements.

3.  A complex situation in which every detail needs to be understood and every "i" dotted and "t" crossed before proceeding.

4.  A set of causal behaviors and events over time that have led to this situation and now might require another set of activities that need to be given time to play out, and probably adjusted, to get the student back on track.

5.  Discerning the student as a member of community now who will contribute to society in the future, and who likely will have his or her own children that may reflect this person's experience in school.

When we asked the teachers which of the five system stories resonated most for them, they were one shy of unanimous that it was story #1. When we asked the administrators which story resonated with them, they were unanimous that it was story #2. And when we asked them all which story represented how decisions would be made in their school, it was unanimous—story #2. Clearly, the system's dynamic was well known and accepted.

Note that, in Hyman Dynamics terms, stories #1 and #2 are both *Emotionally* based. Story #1 is about feelings, making it *Physical-Emotional;* and story #2 is *Mental-Emotional.* Story #3 is a *Mental-Perspective,* and stories #4 & #5 are *Physically* based. And it is story #5 that most aligned with the predominant dynamic in Earth-based cultures.

The primary lesson for the school folks was that in order to have a complete understanding of the human aspects of their system, all 5 perspectives need to be included (and perhaps more).

The lessons for all of us stem from another set of system questions:

→ Does this limited perspective of systems exist throughout education?

→ Is Education a microcosm of society at large?

→ If so, what happens over decades and generations when this limited perspective is virtually always operative?

→ Hasn't the time arrived when we need to have story #5, with its focus on helping students prepare for a life of 'doing the right thing', be a primary teaching/learning experience?

### Achieving Consensus

Among earth-based Indigenous peoples, Nature is a primary teacher, offering insights as well as knowledge; understanding as well as skill. And, in most Indigenous communities, the Talking Circle is used for group decision-making, as a way of speaking and listening, and valuing every voice. The Talking Circle protocol is very simple: one person speaks and all listen respectfully. Often a special object is held by the person speaking, sometimes called a "talking stick," to indicate which person's voice may be heard.

In a Talking Circle, the expectation is that each person is speaking from their heart as well as their mind, and that those present are listening with their hearts as well as their minds, laying aside any previously held notions, ideas, or positions as they listen, and being open to new ways of seeing and understanding in the process.

Jeff's Goebel's 100% Consensus process[51] is unique in that for it, too, Nature is a primary teacher and Talking Circle protocols are closely adhered to for speaking, listening, and valuing every voice.

In this practice Jeff:

→ Has developed a sequence of inquiries that awaken the brain to wanting to solve the problems at hand, and clear the barriers that are perceived and inhibit action;

→ Maintains a focus on our aspirations so that we don't waste energy reacting to negative happenings in our lives;

→ Assures that all the key stakeholders in the project at hand are welcomed to participate, and interviews them in such a way as to influence them to think and act communally;

→ Knows that the slow way is the fast way, and that the time to repair and build relationships may try the patience of most of us Western task oriented, but the relationships are essential;

→ Looks to Nature for appropriate examples of how we might better flow with her to find the processes we should emulate;

→ Opens the doors to what we can become, as opposed to trying to find commonality; and

→ Helps us all understand that we're in an emergent process that will take us beyond the goals and objectives we might have otherwise previously defined.

Jeff has used this process in dozens of places. Because the process is emergent and often accomplished with Earth-based peoples, participants look to Nature and the wisdom of those close to Nature for solutions, and consistently achieve results of cost savings, better governance, solving of adjacent problems, and returning to more Earth-based ways. For example, when he employed his process with a starving village in Africa, at one point they were challenged to do what they said was impossible—increase food production by 50%. When Jeff returned to the

---

[51] https://www.youtube.com/watch?v=3zhHxgFhyag

village after a subsequent growing season, the emergent process they'd created had increased food production by 78%.

Here are the interview questions and topics Jeff uses for the key participants in each *100% Consensus* project:

1) Introductions (as a grounding)
2) What is the situation as you see it, and how do you feel about it?
3) What are the worst possible outcomes of the situation if it is not resolved?
4) Reflect back on what you heard.
5) What are the best possible outcomes that you want to see result from confronting this situation?
6) What could be done to meet the needs of all the parties?
7) What is your advice about who else we should interview?
8) What conditions would facilitate your, or others', participation in resolving this situation?
9) Do you have any questions?
10) Closure – how do you feel about the interview and what did you learn that will help you be successful?

Jeff says that sometimes there is a profound shift in the Interview process when interviewees confide that they are looking for an opportunity to end conflict and their role in its festering and escalation. He says there are two distinctly different types of stories told in the process—the first that is reactive to current situations, and the second that orients us to our aspirations. Folks from empire-based Modernity culture tend to be more reactive and short sighted, while Indigenous peoples take a longer perspective (e.g., 7 generations) and are more oriented to aspirations and guiding principles.

In Modernity culture there is also a phenomenon where anyone can be a victim, which seems to be instrumental in people being reactive. And it affects us all, regardless of our understanding.

As an example, Ruth was on a vacation, scheduled to visit a city she'd studied as a girl and had wanted to visit all her life. At the last minute someone asked to go along on the one day that she would be able to tour the city. It turned out to be a cold, rainy day, and though Ruth had dressed for it, her companion had not, so they modified Ruth's plan to allow for being warm and dry. Then, suddenly, the companion panicked, thinking they didn't have the full day after all, but must be back at their starting point 3 hours earlier than Ruth had planned. She was so insistent that Ruth gave in and they returned—to find that they were, in fact, back 3 hours earlier than necessary, which was too short a time for Ruth to go back into town and see what had been missed. Ruth was fuming; her long-awaited, carefully-planned experience had been ruined. She blamed her companion for "stealing the city" from her. It took many hours of contemplation, and some vigorous exercise, for her to accept her role in the situation.

In another example, Milt was recently on a call sponsored by the *Wisdom Weavers of the World*[52], where one of the topics was, 'Don't React:' keep your attention on aspirations and guiding principles. A couple days later the impeachment process for President Trump was going off the rails and he delivered his State of the Union message, saying things to which Milt reacted strongly. He went to bed quite upset, but woke up thinking abut the *Wisdom Weaver* call, and refocused on this work, as it's grounded in aspirations and guiding principles. He also thought about others who wake up many mornings having experienced profound disappointment, but whose wisdom has somehow transcended the pain. Milt's whole way of being shifted as he felt a strong surge of resilience. Such is the power of mindful action.

## Releasing the Pain of the Past

In western Modernity culture, acquiring and controlling are the norm, and this applies to experiences as well as land, relationships, and material objects. We are trained to acquire and accumulate experiences, and then hold on to whatever memories and reminders of those experiences that we can. When we do this with happy experiences, we may feel as if we are blessed indeed.

---

[52] https://www.wisdomweavers.world/

When we hold on to painful experiences, however, we tend to identify ourselves as victims, and the rest of the world as potential perpetrators.

Eastern and Indigenous cultures offer a different understanding. The film *Dakota 38*[53], a documentary of the Lakota People riding to Mankato, Minnesota for the anniversary of the hanging of 38 warriors in 1863, is an example. In the video their leader, Jim Miller, tells the other riders, 'When we get to Mankato, we're going to apologize to the White people.' The incident had festered and escalated for over 150 years, and the Lakota, as a spiritual people, decided they would take the first step to cleanse it. The mayor of Mankato also had an apology to the Lakota riders, and very heartwarming forgiveness and reconciliation flowed.

## *Ho'oponopono*

Another example of how Indigenous peoples encourage releasing and cleansing rather than holding on to painful memories is the Hawaiian tradition of *Ho'oponopono*. It's an ancient process, perhaps as old as Hawaiian culture. And, as with most Indigenous languages, the sound has power in alignment with the word's meaning: *ho'o* means "to make, to build, to create," while *pono* means "right, correct, fitting." The repeating of *pono* in the word *Ho'oponopono* implies a multi-leveled correction, a restoration.

Among Hawaiians, whenever a disagreement becomes a problem, or there's an injury of any type, an elder calls the people involved together in front of their family and friends. There, they're encouraged to tell their story, to describe in detail what happened and how they felt, until they have been drained of the anger and the hurt. At that point the elder performs a releasing ritual, tells the people involved to express the love that they have for each other and their community, and then declares the whole thing finished. Often a party ensues to ensure that all involved in the process experience the truth and bounty of their shared love.

---

[53] https://www.youtube.com/watch?v=1pX6FBSUyQI

The idea of *Ho'oponopono* was made popular among Americans when Dr. Hew Len, a Hawaiian psychotherapist, was documented[54] as using a version of the practice with inmates in a psychiatric prison in his book. As the story goes, without ever seeing or speaking with a patient, he sat with each inmate's file performing the *Ho'oponopono* ritual, which has been shorthanded into a set of statements: "I am sorry. Please forgive me. I love you. Thank you." Of course, the words in English are not nearly enough to explain the process, because it's not the words that accomplish the results, but the *feeling* they refer to. The first statement is an acknowledgement that there is an imbalance, a disharmony, and that we are party to it. The last is a recognition that we have felt the release and are grateful and appreciative that harmony has been restored.

When Milt had the opportunity to participate with Hawaiians in *Ho'oponopono*, he observed that forgiveness flowed more easily and deeply than it flows in our culture. He asked the ceremonial leaders if they could explain why, and they credited it to the ceremony to which he agreed, but asked if maybe there was something we didn't understand in the Hawaiian culture. He suggested it might be something like a knowing that Earth was given to us in balance and harmony, and if we disrupt the serenity that flows from that knowing, we feel the need to clean up the dissonance we've created. Both parties have this knowing, and so the forgiveness becomes very mutual.

### Forgive Aught Against Any – Ruth

Years ago, after a couple decades of being pushed to accomplish all that western Modernity culture was insisting upon, my body gave out. Doctors were little help in addressing the myriad symptoms, the strange weakness, the pain, and the internal bleeding that would, if unchecked, kill me. Part of me was tired enough to let that happen, but I had children and believed it wouldn't be fair to them if I simply gave up. So, when I was able, I studied and learned and began to understand that there is a direct

---

[54] https://bluebottlelove.com/hew-len-hooponopono/

connection between the condition of the mind and the health of the body.[55]

Perhaps the most important discovery I made in that process was the role of truly releasing and forgiving—myself and everyone else involved in—every painful or upsetting experience I remembered. Catherine Marshall pointed the way, in her book *Something More*, as she described how she overcame a diagnosis of TB and moved on from the years of bedrest she'd been through when she began to write letters to everyone she had any upset feelings about, forgiving and asking forgiveness. The lessons and text of *A Course In Miracles* explained how it worked, that when we let go of our upsets we can fill that space with the love and wellbeing that is our essence and birthright. The practice of *Reiki* helped me experience the free flow of healing energy in and through the body, restoring balance and harmony among the cells and tissues—and to see where blocks remained that needed to be released and forgiven.

Through all these processes I learned that the ideas and beliefs I had built around those painful experiences had not only shaped my thoughts and actions but were actually affecting the cells in my body. The principles of yoga, Unity, and the Science of Mind gave me ideas to replace the old thoughts and reinforce a healthy way of being.

The effects were pronounced, and almost immediate. Each time I did a releasing-snd-replacing process I was stronger and more able to do my work in the world, including mothering my children. Soon, I was helping others with this process, and over the years my mind and body began to work harmoniously together. Now the process I used is written up in several books[56] and an outline is in the Appendix to this book.

---

[55] The full story of Ruth's process is described in her book *Finding the Path, a healing journey,* WiseWoman Press, 2007. Her later understanding of how it works is explained in *The Science of Mental Healing*, Portal Center Press, 2018.

[56] Most completely as one of several mind-body medical method in *Empowered Care,* co-authored with Robert Bruce Newman, and as an

## Rediscovering Our Deepest Truths

*...The dialogic mind is not only a guardian of liberty, but metaphorically similar to a democratic state.*

- *It rejects the tyranny of a single system or dogma;*
- *it welcomes new ideas and guarantees them equality as it considers them;*
- *it provides an open forum for competing theories and systems;*
- *it refuses to censor "dangerous" ideas;*
- *it cherishes and protects its capacity to learn and grow;*
- *it guards as something precious its own access to joy and laughter.*

*~ Robert Grudin[57]*

As we seek the deep underlying truths upon which different cultures and the differences within cultures can come to agreement, we enter into a dialogic process in which the heart and the mind complement each other and function as one. Then thinking and feeling are in harmony, and we are able to embody what it is to be deeply connected.

Ilarion Merculieff is quite adamant that one of the transitions that cultures made when they disconnected from Earth is that their decision-making shifted from the heart to the mind. The problem is that the mind deceives—it justifies, rationalizes, and even changes a memory of an experience—while the heart is an instrument of truth; it never lies. Modernity cultures, however, tend to think of the heart as an instrument of feeling associated most often with an emotion they call love.

This may be related to the change in language that empire-based cultures experienced when they disconnected from Nature. As described earlier, 'love' is a power endowed in the Creation process and perpetuated in Earth-based languages, as such it is a gift experience by all life and that is integral to Earth-based

---

emotional booster in *Making The World Go Away,* both published by Portal Center Press.

[57] Robert Grudin, *On Dialogue*, Houghton Mifflin, 1996, p. 5

cultures appreciating life. From that perspective, the emotions we feel are positive when we feel loved, and negative when love is absent or expressed as hate or disapproval.

Robert Grudin's quote, above, describes how the heart and the mind, along with other sensing organs, work harmoniously in an ongoing internal dialogue. In that way they adhere to the Natural processes described by quantum physics. Humans seem to be the only life form that has created learning which obscures the interconnectedness of quantum reality. With the rediscovery of that reality, along with the shifts toward relationship and process that understanding it requires, the processes of discerning Nature as a mentor and model, designing for emergence, and assuming cooperation as our preferred way of being will all flow more easily.

## Telling Our Stories – Milt

*The shortest distance between a person and their truth is their story.*

~ *Michale Gabriel*[58]

I was quite struck by the above quote when I first heard it; I experienced both resonance and dissonance. The resonance came from the recognition that stories are an integral part of our how we discern ourselves as well as the developing of relationships as we share and often integrate our stories with others as they tell theirs. The dissonance came, and has increased over the years, as I listen to others tell their stories and replay my own; I recognize that I'm not living the story I want to be living. It doesn't always represent who I truly wish to be.

As you can tell from reading this book, I'm in the process of changing that portion of my story for which I feel dissonance, finding more resonance in the Indigenous story.

It's clear to me that if we are to address the issues that underlie the crises we face in the world today, the work to be done is to change our own stories and then figure out how to help

---

[58] Machale Gabriel, presentation as Antioch University OSR Guest Faculty, 2002.

others be ready and able to change their story, as well. Our intent is to find a common narrative that blends the Modernity ways into Earth-based ways, and when I reflect on Jeff Goebel's *100% Consensus* work that's exactly what he's doing. How else would he get 100% consensus from people coming from very divergent perspectives, often emanating from deeply held beliefs?

Goebel's 100% Consensus can be achieved because, in spite of our differences, we are all the same in terms of our source. We come from stardust; we are alive; and we are human. In interfaith circles it is often said as, "We are all one; we are all interconnected."

Yet, coming from different cultures we think, act, and process quite differently. When we begin to accept that life can be experienced in different ways with equal validity, we begin to be open to a whole new level of life and learning.

Isn't the cultural norm we're seeking found in both the commonness we share and the diversity that often attracts us and is necessary for addressing our current dilemma?

The Hopi Prophesy described above is a story, and our interpretations of it represent other stories. In Thomas King's *The Truth About Stories*, he tells us a Native American creation story followed by his interpretation of the King James Version of "Adam and Eve," the Judeo-Christian creation story. And when he's done he compares the two renditions:

> A theologian might argue that these two creation stories are essentially the same. Each tells about the creation of the world and the appearance of human beings. But a storyteller would tell you that these two stories are quite different, for whether you read the Bible as sacred text or secular metaphor, the elements in Genesis create a particular universe governed by a series of hierarchies – God, man, animals, plants – that celebrate law, order, and good government, while in our Native story, the universe is governed by a series of co-operations – Charm, the Twins, animals, humans – that celebrate equality and balance.[59]

---

[59] Thomas King, *The Truth About Stories*, Super Summary, 2003.

I think it is also fair to say that not only are the Creation stories different because of who is telling them, but they are received in vastly different ways based on the language spoken by the listener. And, as with so many differences in understanding, these vastly different ways may be expressed in terms of cultural norms and consciousness.

In my Jewish congregation we may read Genesis occasionally, but the story reflected in our prayers and our psyche is the Exodus story, with its laws and commandments that lead us to focus on social order rather than ecological integrity. This isn't surprising when we discern the Ten Commandments are essentially a social contract. They tell us who we should be in relationship with one another in the present moment.

Being sustainable, on the other hand, requires that we have a strong ethic regarding both

→ Who we are for the Earth, and

→ Who we are for future generations.

And neither of these is addressed in Moses' Law or the stories that explain and support it. In today's world, we need a different kind of story—with a different set of guiding principles.

Another story exemplifies how studying the Ancient Hebrew profoundly changed my connection to Judaism. One of my attempts to learn more led me to a class taught by Rabbi Jack Gabriel. He told a story of leading a small synagogue where the children attended class while Shabbat services were being held, and he would excuse himself for a few minutes from the service to visit each class. The children were very important to him and he always prepared for the classes. Except for one week, where every plan to prepare was interrupted, and he ended up in class unprepared. So he improvised and found himself saying, "Today we're going to do a Jewish Haiku."

He just got through explaining the 5-syllable, 7-syllable, 5-syllable rhythm of the three line poem, and a bright young student, Isaac, jumped up, "I got one! I got it!" And the Rabbi asked him to relax while he explained more about the organic flow of Haiku. But Isaac was relentless, and so the Rabbi said, "OK

Isaac, what's your Haiku?" and Isaac recited what is a most sacred Hebrew prayer: The *Shema*.

Our class with the Rabbi was also given the assignment of writing a Jewish Haiku, and Isaac's understanding and mine are both shown below.

| Hebrew Prayer | Transliteration | Translation |
|---|---|---|
| שמע ישראל<br>יי אלהינו<br>יי אחד | Sh'ma Yisrael<br>Adonoi Elohanu<br>Adonoi Echad | Hear O'Israel<br>The Lord is our God<br>The Lord is One |

### Milt's Haiku

**Feel the Covenant
That Creates and Sustains Life
Omnipresent Source**

(I wonder if perhaps there isn't a sacred poetry to which people who are deeply connected with the Earth are attuned?)

Based on these and other experiences, I've come to believe that, by learning from others, and with a clear intention on our own part, any of us who wish to can participate in and shape a desired culture based on our most cherished virtues. These authentic bridging stories may help many others find a more appropriate path for theselves.

## Acting on Principle

### Goals or Principles?

Since the consciousness that caused a problem is insufficient for addressing it, and the consciousness we're talking about is integral to our cultural meme, there's a need to look at what might be regarded a 'sacred cows' regarding Climate Change and Sustainability. Two in particular are *The Earth Charter: Values and*

*Principles for a Sustainable Future*[60] and the *United Nations 17 Sustainable Development Goals (SDGs)*[61].

When he first learned of the *Earth Charter,* Milt was thrilled to have a document that was oriented to guiding principles, and he bought 100 copies to distribute to others. There is one shortfall of the document, though, and that is the weakness of the statement made regarding the Indigenous peoples, which says:

*Affirming the right of indigenous peoples to their spirituality, knowledge, lands and resources and to their related practice of sustainable livelihoods.*

This statement needs to be amended to include also:

*... and listening, learning, and beginning to embody all that the Indigenous peoples know about living in relationship with our beautiful planet so that we might once again live in ecological and social balance and harmony.*

The *UN 17 Goals* (detailed later in this book) highlight a different issue. Modernity culture's orientation toward goals keeps us from designing for emergence—hence missing opportunities for possible solutions we hadn't begun to consider. We plan based on specific tasks rather than focus on relationship and process, so our strategic plans are often the steps we need to take to achieve our goals. Efforts to work harmoniously with Nature, however, must be guided by aspirations and principles that then allow us to flow past whatever we may have initially defined as our goals to discover what is really possible.

Having Earth-based people guide us through these processes will benefit us in many ways, such as experiencing relational leadership and recognizing that what may appear as a duality between planning based on goals or based on principles, can be readily integrated. Organizing relationally vs. hierarchically may be an example of duality, but the real issue is not the structure, but which is the primary organizing principle. The Indigenous way is

---

[60] https://earthcharter.org/read-the-earth-charter/
[61] https://www.un.org/sustainabledevelopment/sustainable-development-goals/

to be primarily relational, and then to utilize hierarchy to lead certain projects, after which the leaders enter back into non-hierarchical community, when the need for such leadership is complete.

When a small group that I worked with at Portland State University (PSU) was asked if we could design a Colloquium to fill in for a cancellation less than three weeks in the future, a topic and design came immediately to mind for me. One of the folks in the group, Jim Newcomer, had just been telling us about a very bright individual who was espousing that, *"we have ravaged, wasted, polluted and past so many tipping points, there is no way to save for us to survive."* I said to Jim, "Do you think, if we use the Curve of Hope graphic and get your friend to be the first speaker; together select a second speaker who is responsible for developing sustainable solutions, and I find someone to articulate what it is to live in balance and harmony with Earth—have we got a program?"

He was interested so we explored a little about who the second person might be and who would follow up, and then I said that the third person must be Indigenous, and must speak last. We'd show them the curve, but not coach them at all. It was a go.

The Colloquium began with introductions and showing the following graph. The first speaker was asked to talk about the impacts of the 'Waste & Pollution Curve'; the second speaker, the Director of the PSU Institute for Sustainable Solutions, would talk about necessary 'Exponential Improvements'; and the third, Unangan Elder Ilarion Merculioff, the balance and harmony found in 'The Curve of Hope'.

The Curve of Hope
Waste & Pollution Curve
Exponential Improvements

The first speaker essentially said, "We've passed so many tipping points, you can kiss your grandkids goodbye."

The second speaker chose to articulate potential success in terms of developing a shared vision with a plan that focused on goals, objectives, measurements, and milestones rather than what we labeled "Exponential Improvements."

And the third speaker eloquently enlightened all of us. His perspective of being in ecological and social harmony is based on principles, ethics, and virtues that are timeless. The virtues of the past that have been lived for centuries are the same virtues we want for our children and all the generations that follow, and in order to achieve these virtues, he reiterated several times, we must live them every day.

The stark contrast between the second speaker's approach developing a plan with goals, objectives, measurements and milestones, and that third speaker's approach of guiding principles awakened me to a major difference in our cultures, and it's the latter that continue to resonate deeply. I'm now much more aware of how goals and objectives often obscure our guiding principles.

*It's all so simple.*

*~ Dené Elder Be'sha Blondin*[62]

I heard Be'sha speak these words at a workshop in Portland not long after the colloquium described above. I was struck by the truth, and the paradox, in them. After some consideration, I believe that she was saying that the guiding principles which are strictly followed by Earth cultures, when applied to what appear to Modernity culture to be complex problems, make the answer to those problems readily apparent.

---

[62] Dene Elder Be'sha Blondin,  Sahtu Region of NW Territories, Canada, commenting on the complexity of our work

## Learning & Teaching

### Pedagogical Comparisons—Milt

In 2009 I attended The Parliament of the World's Religions in Melbourne, Australia. I was drawn to the conference when I heard that the Aboriginal People of Australia were integral to its design and facilitation, and I went with one burning question:

*How do they teach their children so that they understand and practice all that is essential to life and to their culture?*

I was not disappointed, and when I returned to Portland I enrolled in classes at Portland State University's Native American Studies program, led by Dr. Cornel Pewewardy. I developed the following chart for one of my classes and Cornel introduced me to Patrick Eaglestaff, Principal of The Native American Youth and Family Center (NAYA). It is partially through observing the successes of NAYA that I have grown to better understand how our education can be greatly improved.

So, when State standards were received by the Merlo Station Community High School in Beaverton, Oregon, the Principal, Dr. Jean Pence, asked me if I'd work with three teachers who had said to her, 'This is the antithesis of everything we're trying to do at Merlo Station,' I agreed and met with the teachers monthly for the school year. They articulated their vision, purpose, and principles, and then explained the dissonance that the standards created. The purpose of the school was primarily to serve students who'd not done well in the school system—specifically on tests. The standards were in the form of a test to be taken by sophomores, and passing the test was mandatory for the students to graduate. We worked on putting together a case to achieve a waiver from having to pass the test to graduate.

We also did something else that helped me understand standards and our current education philosophy. I asked the three teachers to read the standards for 5th graders, and when we gathered to discuss them, we all liked them. The two sets of standards, for 5th graders and sophomores, differed in one major respect. The latter were pass/fail, an objective measurement with a lot of issues, and the former were designed to help the teacher and the student recognize the concepts and facts they hadn't comprehended and would likely need to know for future learning. Subsequently I did a short presentation on standards that concluded with the following question:

> Are standards primarily in place to support an improvement process, or is the improvement process in place to support the standards?

A very small sample of educators were split 50-50 on their response and unfortunately what we implemented is the improvement process support the standards.

To me, this seems to inhibit learning being an improvement process in which student exploration can be made around their own interests, emergent processes can be developed, and teachers can be mentors guiding students (and themselves) to explore what they don't know and awaken their already knowing.

The chart on the next page shows that in the United States we originally created public education so that we would have a literate, informed, trained citizenry so that Democracy could thrive. Then, in the Industrial Age, there was a stark shift to provide the skills to support the new found power of the factory. We solidified ourselves as a Knowledge culture, and now are left with the challenge of how to live sustainably on Earth.

As part of a colonizing, empire-based culture, it's sometimes difficult to discern and accept what we have wrought through our initial attempts to assimilate, followed by indifference toward, and now the need to accept Earth-based guiding principles. It takes a paradigm shift to discern ourselves as being birthed to learn and our organizations as living organisms.

Indigenous peoples, on the other hand, maintained their approach of learning from Nature with appreciation for the land and all life, as well as developing the survival skills that are highly dependent on communal relations. They maintained their *Wisdom* culture based on Nature's laws of interdependence, and now as they struggle to overcome the scars of colonization, they are offering to provide the relational leadership so all life might once again flourish. A significant part of this task is to recognize that their pedagogy, based in their own languages, is continually awakening an already knowing.

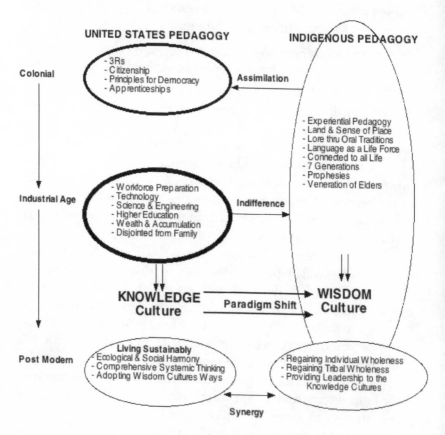

## The Ebb and Flow of Tribal Education

Dr. Gregory Cajete, in his book, *Look to the Mountain: An Ecology of Indigenous Education*, describes a process that he calls "The Ebb and Flow of Tribal Education." As he presents it, the whole process is grounded in Spiritual Ecology, "For Indigenous People, Nature and all it contains formed the parameters of the school," he says, and that school is informed by two very complex, dynamic processes.

His first set of processes consists of:

→ Mythic,

→ Visionary, and

→ Artistic.

These are designed to "develop a deep understanding of the inner being." His second set,

→ Environmental,

→ Affective and

→ Communal,

are "the outward, highly interactive, and external dimension of Tribal education."[63]

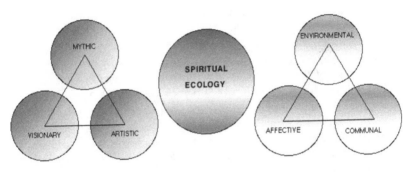

In all this there is a sense of timelessness, an understanding that the cherished virtues, ethics, and guiding principles of the ancestors are the basis of our desired future for the generations that follow, and we must live these virtues every day in order for them to become our reality.

With Spiritual Ecology at the heart of Indigenous education, Nature becomes the mentor and model that is understood in terms of processes and relationships, balance and harmony. Earth becomes *our* steward (in direct contradiction with the Judeo-Christian model, in which humanity is set to steward the Earth), and the relationships between humanity and other Earth beings are mutual and co-creative. The primary thought process is

---

[63] Gregory Cajete, *Look to the Mountain: An Ecology of Indigenous Education*, p. 39 Colorado: Kivakii Press, 1994.

organic rather than mechanical, and the worldview is one of sufficient abundance, where the Earth's capacities to renew, cleanse, and heal are always honored. When given the opportunity to reflect, we can begin to live a form of Sacred Ecology.

This was brought home to Milt while visiting a segment of land purchased by the Portland area Metro governance council:

> It was a combination of farmland, forest and wetlands located about 10 miles south of Portland. The land had been left to its natural ways for a relatively short time and a profusion of native plants had emerged. It appeared that latent seeds that had been dormant for decades now flourished when left alone to do so.

> I'd been told the Metro folks who were our hosts were extremely earthy treehuggers, whose life-work was all about restoration and ecological sustainability. As I walked the land I made a point of walking with Mr. David Lewis, a member of the Confederated Tribes of Grand Ronde, and asked him to share with me what he was thinking and observing. We walked in silence for a time before he shared with me a deep appreciation for Metro and the people who had worked so hard to protect this land and let it flourish naturally. He also expressed that the land without people with an ancestral understanding of the plants and terrain was incomplete. He shared with me how certain plants would be harvested and treated so that they would become a part of village life—medicines, materials for weaving, and all the other functions necessary for humans to flourish while accepting their responsibility for maintaining balance and harmony. David helped me understand how integral human activities are to bringing life to this place, and how there was a sense that perhaps our Modernity culture's sense of preservation had an ornamental feel.

When David spoke of connecting with the land Milt remembered the profound happiness expressed by people he'd observed feeling that connection. Told about the experience later, a Lakota friend said, "That's contentment", and Ilarion Merculieff said, "That's bliss."

The term Spiritual Ecology resonates deeply with these ideas, and with some very similar terminology utilized in Don Beck's Spiral Dynamics. As described above, the essence of Spiral Dynamics is that every culture operates out of one or more 'memes' or mental models of who we are, individually and collectively, in terms of our values, basic worldview and level of consciousness. As individuals and as a culture, we evolve (or devolve) in a spiral process from one meme to another—always including some of what we've learned and practiced from previous memes.

1 BEIGE — survival; biogenic needs satisfaction; reproduction

2 PURPLE — safety/security; protection from harm; family bonds

3 RED — power/action; asserting self to dominate others; control

4 BLUE — stability/order; obedience to earn later reward; meaning

5 ORANGE — opportunity/success; competing to achieve results; influence

6 GREEN — harmony/love; joining together for mutual growth; awareness

7 YELLOW — independence/self-worth; fitting a living system; knowing

8 TURQUOISE — global community/life force; survival of Earth; consciousness

The chart above shows the flow of cultures from top to bottom, and this book is largely about how Modernity culture needs to flow past the Green meme through the Yellow meme, to rediscover the wisdom of interconnectedness. That process requires we develop the basic understanding of the attributes and endowments of living systems as well as the systemic understanding regarding interdependent life processes.

This understanding is integral to Earth-based wisdom and creates the spiritual connection to life that is available to all people by reconnecting with Nature. It's the essence of the Turquoise meme toward which we are striving.

## Ceremony

Because empire-based Modernity culture emphasizes mental and intellectual processes for taking in and processing information, ritual and ceremony are rarely understood, much less applied, as tools for development. In fact, though, we all have rituals; that is, we all have activities that we perform in very much the same way on a regular basis. We have wake-up rituals and going-to-bed rituals; we have ritual greetings and good-byes; we have rituals for starting projects and ending projects—and many more. We also have family rituals: how we eat together, what we say or don't say to each other, what we "always" do together. And we have community and national rituals, when we gather for some meetings, and honor seasons and holidays and powerfully impacting events.

Modernity culture does permit some ceremony. We listen to the national anthem at large gatherings; we celebrate weddings and funerals according to ceremonial guidelines; different religious groups include ceremonies in their gatherings.

However, outside of those religious events, Modernity culture does not encourage a sense of sacredness about these rituals. Nor does Modernity culture recognize the power of a ceremony as a potentially life-changing event—both of which are inherent in the ceremonies and rituals of Earth-based Indigenous cultures.

### Sun Dance—Milt

In the summer of 2013 I was invited to attend a Sun Dance. I want to be very careful what I write, as I believe the Sun Dance to be very sacred, and I was a guest who only scratched the surface regarding what was to be learned. I was very honored, and profoundly changed by the experience.

I arrived at the Sun Dance site the day before the dancing would begin, in order to attend an organizing and information-sharing meeting. When I arrived I could see a large number of tents and tepees grouped around what appeared to be common cooking and gathering areas under canvas covered arbors. I asked one of the security people who checked me in how many people were expected, and he told me over 400. I was amazed, and assumed we would have quite a long meeting. The meeting started at 3pm and covered all that we would need to know about protocols, food, costs, ice deliveries, porta-potties, security, the Moon Lodge, and I can't remember all the other topics. For each topic, someone stood up from the audience and gave a succinct talk on what we needed to know. Often there were concerns shared, like not enough money to cover the costs of the 8 meals served in the communal kitchen, and needing signups for security, etc. And in each case it was assumed that everyone would pitch in to provide whatever support was necessary. The meeting was over before 4:30. I was stunned, and knew that I was part of something very special. It seemed to me that there wasn't a need to dwell on problems because there was a mutual trust in a community who would address any and all issues once they were surfaced.

I left after the meeting to go stay with my daughter's family for the evening and pick up a tent and other supplies that I would need. So I missed the selection and mounting of the sacred tree that would stand at the center of dance arbor, and serve as the focal point for prayers and strength for the dancers.

When I returned, I set up my tent among folks that I mostly knew from the Earth & Spirit Council of Portland. I met some new people, learned more of what to expect, and turned in early as wake-up would be around 5:15am for supporting the Opening Procession at 6:00am.

The Sun Dance lasts for 4 days and the Dancers are both men and women who go without food and water in what turned out to be (and often is) very hot weather—a couple of days it was over 100 degrees. Each day there was an Opening Procession, then four dance rounds, and a Closing Procession.

The dancing was held in a large, open, circular area surrounded by an arbor where the hundreds of supporters could stand and sit, and a separated area for the dancers to rest between rounds. There appeared to be a single dance step repeated over and over again, and there were several men and women in the arbor to support the dancers. I learned that the dancers are dancing more for their People than they are for themselves, and this is why it is so important to be present and support them each time they dance. Male dancers are tethered to the tree through inserts in their chests. Some break free in the round when they are tethered, and some, the Eagle Dancers, are tethered for each round, each day.

What I experienced outside the dance arbor was every bit as informative regarding community and ceremony. Everyone seemed to operate according to guiding principles of helping, sharing, and addressing whatever needs arose. I was helped to understand what to expect and what was expected of me. There was an air of genuine friendliness and caring. I wasn't quite family, but the invitation was there. One of the things I was most impressed with was the openness and trust, as the local cooking and gathering area with all their food and equipment were wide open, and each of the tents and tepees seemed very accessible, while honoring others' privacy. When I later mentioned my observations to a colleague, he mentioned that in a previous year there had been a thief who was caught, and he was embraced by the community in such a way that he was welcome at this year's Sun Dance.

One of the things that I was most taken with among the Dancers was the compassionate support they received and provided to others throughout. As you can imagine in such a physically and emotionally exhausting endeavor, many of the dancers broke down and wept. They were compassionately led to the tree and cared for until they were ready to resume. There seemed to be a guiding principle of keeping every one in the community of dancers and most dancers recovered relatively quickly, while a few others sat out a round or more.

In addition to the 'Prayer Rounds' of the Dance, there were several rounds that seemed life-changing for the participants, and deeply affected me. The first was a Veteran's Round in which both men and women who had served in the military were honored. It was apparent that many of them had carried home deep physical and psychological wounds, and the round was intended for healing. There were emotional breakdowns, and the support from the dancers and fellow veterans never waivered. I saw many of the veterans after the honoring, and spoke with a couple. It was clear that they had had a transformative experience. The second was a Children's Round, with many of the children accompanied by Sun Dance participants. The pride of the parents and the children was palpable. I should also mention that children accompanied by parents or grandparents were included in a round each day.

There was another transformative moment that I'd like to share. It occurred on the 4th day. A Portland Elder, Rod McAfee, who had dealt with severe health challenges for the last years, joined us and was sitting in the front row for a morning round when one of the dancers who had at one time been incarcerated, asked to come see Rod. The Dancer was escorted to where Rod was sitting and thanked Rod for "saving his life." I knew that Rod had worked in the prisons, and assume he had counseled this young man, perhaps run a sweat in the prison.

Rod doesn't hear well these days, and when his wife Linda told him what the Dancer had said, he asked him to come back. The Dancer was escorted back. Rod talked to him for several minutes, and then he was escorted back to the dancer's rest area. I don't think there was a dry eye anywhere. Rod's work in the prison, the Sun Dance, and now Rod's presence in this ceremony all seemed to converge into a moment when Rod, with his wisdom, solidified a life-change for this young man.

Closure for me was complete when, in the last dance round, the Eagle Dancers, surrounded by their community and supported by all the other dancers, broke from their tether. I don't think I can express the incredible pride that emanated from the community. This was followed by the Procession of the Dancers so that we could each see each other in a very close and share a personal salute to all that had transpired.

I had a choice to stay another evening and participate in the next day's feast and give-away or to say my goodbyes, break camp and head for home. I chose the latter because I felt as if I had experienced transformation in a profound way, and I wanted time to reflect. Also, I didn't feel as if I was quite yet 'family' with these wonderful hosts, and perceived the feast and give-away to be 'family' events.

I came away with the realization that transformation through ceremony is the norm in many cultures. What I learned through experiencing it is how very real it is, and that it is accessible to all of us if we just want to incorporate it for fulfilling lifecycle events and invoking necessary life changes.

In addition, my Sun Dance experience is one of hope. Unfortunately, the U.S. government banned these Native ceremonies from the late 1800s until quite recently. The Sun Dance that I attended is less than 20 years old, but already we are seeing the positive effects, as children who attended the first Sun Dances are now coming of age and marrying, having children, and participating in both the community and as dancers.

Both before and after this experience I spoke with several people who've struggled in empire-based society about their experience being on 'The Red Road'. They'd found a path for themselves through ceremonies that are grounded in an appreciation and gratitude for life, ecological integrity, family, and community.

## For Reflection

> Think about a time in your life when you heard someone share something that was a truth for them, but was nothing you'd ever experienced and was foreign to your understanding of life, but it opened a new possibility for you, and you found you wanted to know more—perhaps even integrate it into you own beliefs. An example of such an event happened for Milt when he heard that his grandmother who lived in Portland awoke in the middle of the night knowing that her mother in Russia had just passed away, and two weeks later they got a message that her mother had died—at the same time she had awakened.

> ➤ If you are with a group, pair up with one other person and take a few minutes to share your stories; then meet back with the group to share what you experienced. Experience has consistently shown that a feeling emerges of being very much in relationship as the sharing is real and intimate. Participants often have found a new friend, and these conversations have led to other trusting conversations and actions.

# 7. Hope

*Never let your People lose hope.*

*~ Chief Lyons*[64]

This writing is intended to be more than a book. It is a hopeful plan with an invitation to join like-hearted people—through the internet as well as in local groups.

Yet it's being written in a time when many people in empire-based Modernity culture are feeling a sense of hopelessness. We, the authors, believe the underlying reason for that hopelessness is that, while we've been taught that we control our destiny and the processes that affect that destiny, we don't control this virus—or the climate change that some believe contributed to its spread.

Nature, however, does. Earth-based cultures know this, and they also know that Nature has given them all the gifts and lessons necessary to not only survive, but to flourish. In gratitude for these lessons and gifts, they flow with Nature, and maintain a covenant of mutual support.

The graph below extends the one offered earlier in this book, showing what can happen to our populations if we begin to adopt and adapt the guiding principles of Earth-based peoples into our daily life. It's clear that the experience of empire-based culture is really a small, but powerful blip in the history of humanity on this planet. It decimated the cultures that were solely reliant on Nature as their teacher/mentor/guide.

But because of what has been accomplished by the empires, a new kind of culture is emerging, one that operates in harmony with Nature while using the powerful tools that the empire-based culture developed, so the population of humanity can thrive for generations to come.

Accomplishing this, moving beyond the current distress of our past 'lose/lose' games, requires grace—the grace to change

---

[64] of the Turtle Clan of the Seneca Nations of the Iroquois Confederacy

our story about domination that has obscured the ecological and communal guiding principles that are so necessary for life to flourish.

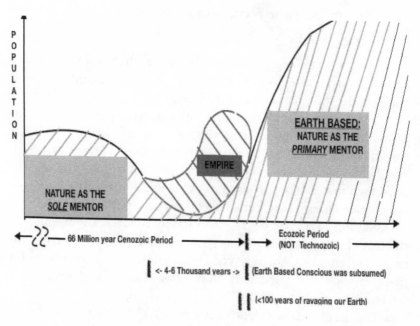

## A False Sense of Hope

There is a caveat to messages of hope: we must not want it so badly that we accept false hope. Currently the dominant societies hold technology as our greatest hope. Surely our best technology is necessary because of the urgency and severity of our problems – a decade or less to be on a path of flowing with Nature. Yet, after decades of observation we, the authors, have come to see that while modern technology is necessary, it's not sufficient; it may deal with specific problems, but leaves us with the same ethical dilemma that caused those problems.

It's true that, for a large percentage of the human population, life is easier, more comfortable, healthier—and longer—than ever before. On the next page are a few graphs to illustrate that fact: And all this is great! We're delighted that so many more people are happier and healthier than a couple centuries ago!

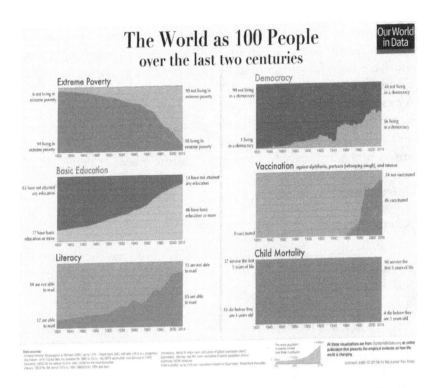

Still, we're not convinced that these indicators are valid for the long haul—we're not sure they are sustainable.

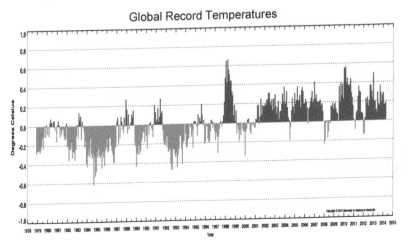

Rising global temperatures are the number-one indicator of that concern. Scientists have reported on the issue of increased surface tempreatures and related climate change since the 1970s, but have been largely ignored by policymakers in government and business. As a result, each year we've seen record high temperatures, all over the planet.

We're also beginning to see greater droughts in some areas and more damaging storms and flooding in others—all of which are significant threats to Modernity culture's way of living, which is not in harmony with Earth's processes, and so, by definition, is unstable and unsustainable.

## Sustainability

Over nearly 30 years the United Nations has been working toward planetary sustainability and in 2015 established its 17 Sustainability Goals for the world. These include:

At last count, over a thousand governmental and nongovernmental agencies and organizations and perhaps millions of well intentioned individuals around the world are focusing on these goals. A few of them have been working since the 1970s. They're working very hard, and have had many small successes; yet our planet continues to experience the greatest mass extinction of species in millions of years, and human habitation continues to be increasingly difficult in more and more places. Sadly, their work is not accomplishing what we all have hoped. The problem, and a possibile solution, is laid out by Michael Dowd and Katharine Hayhoe in their video: "Ask Philanthropists: Sound Alarm Now!"[65]

## An Ancient Way of Thinking

The lack of success by Modernty culture organizations in turning this huge process around is clearly not a function of lack of ability; we have the tools and the wealth, and even the healthy populations, to do whatever is necessary. No, the problem is not lack of capacity or of technology—it's a lack of will or, in the terminology of our Indigenous mentors, of spirit. And that, we believe, is a function of a mindset that cannot perceive the underlying issue, essential processes, and fundamental principles

Equally clearly, there is a mindset, a paradigm, that can perceive these issues and processes, and it is built into the language and culture of Earth-based Indigenous peoples. In Ilarion Merculieff's Native Perspectives video, *Sustainability,*[66] he informs us that there is no Unangan word for sustainability—his people embody it. As Milt has observed Merculieff over the years, he has come to understand that, because the Unangans have retained their connection with Earth, they're very clear about the set of life processes with which all living systems have been blessed. More, he's seen that such cultural wisdom is embedded in their language in a way that's very similar to Carlo Suarez' Ancient Hebrew matrix described earlier in this book. This mindset is expressd in the profound wisdom of the Earth-based prophets, like Chief Seattle.

*Tribe follows tribe, and nation follows nation, like the waves of the sea.*
*It is the order of nature, and regret is useless.*
*Your time of decay may be distant, but it will surely come*

---

[65] https://youtu.be/1V8PdnNoEio
[66] https://www.youtube.com/watch?v=4h6uxDQWb3U

*for even the White Man whose God walked and talked with him as friend to friend, cannot be exempt from the common destiny.*
*We may be brothers after all.*

*~Chief Seattle, Suquamish Nation, 1854*[67]

We now must heed the messages of the prophets of our own time that recognize that our disconnection from Nature a few thousand years ago caused us to lose sight of the endowments all life was blessed with at Creation. A few of many, many notable works include (in no particular order)

→ Rachel Carson's *Silent Spring,*
→ Lyn Margulis'[68] & James Lovelock's *The Gaia Hypothesis,*
→ Fritjof Capra's *The Web of Life* and *The Hidden Key*
→ Berry & Swimme's *Universe Story,*
→ James Carse's *Finite and Infinite Games,*
→ Janine Beynus's *BioMimicry,*
→ Robin Wall Kimmerer's *Braiding Sweetgrass*
→ Otto Scharmer's *Theory U.*
→ Peter Senge's. *The 5th Discipline: The Art and Practice of the Learning Organization*
→ Sandra Seagal's *Human Dynamics*
→ Michael Dowd's *Thank God for Evolution*

Two such authors who write of the importance of discerning Earth as alive and vibrant are Joanna Macy and Peter Senge, and their statements provide some energy for pulling us into our future:

*The greatest revolution of our time is in the way we see the world. The mechanistic paradigm underlying the Industrial Growth Society gives way to the realization that we belong to a living, self- organizing cosmos… This realization changes everything.*

---

[67] https://suquamish.nsn.us/home/about-us/chief-seattle-speech/
[68] https://www.youtube.com/watch?v=ILU_--jxO5U

*It changes our perceptions of who we are and what we need, and how we can trustfully act together for a decent, noble future.*

   ~Joanna Macy[69]

*I believe we can start to discern three elements of much deeper changes becoming evident. The first comes from seeing knowledge and knowledge creation as the is the cornerstone of what makes any organization successful..... The second comes from seeing all organizations embedded in and interdependent with larger natural and social systems...... the third element. How work is organized must be guided by principles of living systems.*

*Together these three elements could be the basis for a second industrial revolution that would close the circle and enable humans to live once again as part of, rather than apart from, nature.*

   ~Peter Senge[70]

As we begin to understand living systems, one of their most intriguing qualities is *Emergence*, and it is a quality on which hope depends because it allows us to flow to ways of being that are far beyond what we can define as goals or objectives.

Milt describes his own learning that brought him to writing this book as a story of emergence:

→ getting involved in sustainability,
→ knowing he needed to understand living systems,
→ discovering that all life is endowed with life processes,
→ finding those processes imbedded in living languages, and then
→ incorporating them in an exercise to help people understand and embody paradigm shifts.

And just as that exercise awakened an already-knowing for him, when he shared it with students, it awakened a similar knowing in

---

[69] https://www.joannamacy.net/
[70] Peter Senge, Foreword to *Profit Beyond Measure*, by Anders Bröms and H. Thomas Johnson, Free Press, 2008, p. xvi.

them. That exercise is a bridge that helps folks understand better what Earth-based culture know intuitively, and as we tell our stories, other bridges will emerge to help folks better understand reality beyond Newtonian physics, relational leadership, creating win/win situations, the energetic connections carried through languages of life, and more.

Designing for emergence is instrumental in the three tools we've offered in this book: *Talking Circles, 100% Consensus* and *Appreciative Inquiry.* Conveners of such processes say that it has never failed them, and when we're introduced to this collaborative way of being, we get a glimpse of its power to resolve differences and lead to the creation of something new, something that never existed before.

## Hero's Journey

*The Hero's Journey is a classic story structure that's shared by stories worldwide. Coined by academic Joseph Campbell in 1949, it refers to a wide-ranging category of tales in which a character ventures out to get what they need, faces conflict, and ultimately triumphs over adversity.*[71]

Like so many things in life, might we look at Climate Change as both a curse and a blessing. The blessing is that it unifies all of us to be on our common hero's journey—a journey that began with Creation and established the flourishing truths of life. We've disrupted the process, but there is real hope, when we rediscover ancient truths of living in balance and harmony with the life-renewing processes bestowed to all life millions of years ago and then flowing with Nature. This discovery is available to us through the stories of those who've lived the ancient truths, and we can allow them to awaken the already-knowing that resides in each of us.

To fulfill that journey, however, we must remain disciplined to accepting reality of our living planet and our culpability in its

---

[71] Jul 20, 2018; https://www.google.com/search?client=firefox-b-1-d&q=hero%27s+journey

potential destruction. This is made starkly clear by the message of Ilarion Merculieff's understanding of his role as *Kuuyux*.

> *My traditional name is Kuuyux, given to me by the last Kuuyux amongst my people, the Unangan, (Aleut), when I was 4. It means something like: an arm extended out from the body, a carrier of ancient knowledge, a messenger. Now, I am living that legacy and I carry messages from Indigenous Elders from many cultures. It is my mission, it is my passion, it is who I am.*[72]

According to Earth-based prophesies, and confirmed by Western science, we have less than a decade to reverse the processes that have destroyed global ecological processes and communal guiding principles. Ilarion has recently stated that he will be the last Kuuyux because the time has come when we either address Climate Change successfully or perish, and in either case there is no longer a need for him to select a successor.

Dr. Richard Tarnas suggests in his article, "Romancing the Cosmos,"[73] that the possibility exists to reframe our destiny. He writes that our universe is "a deeply-souled, subtly mysterious cosmos of great spiritual beauty and creative intelligence." He goes on to create an understanding that when we view the cosmos 'as being at least as intelligent and noble, as worthy a being, as permeated with mind and soul, as imbued with moral aspiration and purpose, as endowed with spiritual depths and mystery' as we are, then we might find the mutuality to unite 'and thereby bring forth something new, a creative synthesis'. Dr. Tarnas suggests that what emerges may be a new capacity for self-transcendence, both intellectual and moral, so that we may experience a new dimension of beauty and intelligence in the world—not a projection of our own desire for beauty and intellectual mastery, but an encounter with the actual unfolding beauty, unpredictability, and intelligence of the whole.[39]

Although we've been taught otherwise, we are human beings, part of the system we call Earth, and therefore capable of

---

[72] https://www.wisdomweavers.world/meet-the-core-team
[73] Richard Tarnas, "Romancing the Cosmos," *IONS Shift* 12/2005–2/2006

grounding our lives in the appreciation, gratitude, and acceptance of our responsibility to be in concert with the Earth as it cleanses and heals to provide pristine water, air, and soil so life forms of all kinds might flourish.

## For Reflection

➤ What part of your journey benefits someone(s) or some other form of life?

➤ How is that part of 'paying forward' or contributing to a paradigm shift?

➤ Is there an awakening that's influenced your journey?

➤ Is there another awakening you'd like to have? How will you find it?

➤ How would such an awakening influence your actions with regard to life on this planet?

# 8. Moving Forward

*You can't organize this,.*
*If there's not spirit, it won't happen.*

~ *Lakota Elder Alberta Iron Cloud Miller* [74]

Humanity is at that very point in time when a 4000-year-old era is dying and another is struggling to be born—a shifting of culture, science, society, and institutions enormously greater than the world has ever experienced.

We now recognize the urgent and critical nature of global climate change, and that we must prepare for very difficult times ahead. And we should recognize that the majority of systemic understanding and leadership in protecting life's most precious natural gifts is coming from Indigenous peoples. Their voices are yearning to be heard. And the work of Modernity culture must be to refocus all of the well meaning individuals and organizations to ensure the same systemic understanding that informs us all of the changes we need to make, and Modernity must reach a point where they listen, learn, continue to search for cornerstones of the ancient cultures, and then trust that other's have the processes to provide relational leadership to our desired future.

There is not time for missteps or delay. The steps we've taken and those that now guide the work that needs to be done are shown in the graphic below, which we're repeating from our exploration of the Hopi Prophecy, back in chapter 3.

Starting at the circle on the left and moving in a clockwise direction, we've written about the time when it was recognized that the Earth's systems were alive and Nature was our sole mentor, and with the separation from Earth came hierarchical institutions that have led to our ethical shortfall. With this realization we began building bridges so we might better

---

[74] Advice from Lakota Elder Alberta Ironcloud Miller, when Milt was trying to restructure a failing project.

understand Earth-based ways, and found that learning about living systems resonated deeply and awakened an understanding of the paradigm shifts that people want to make individually as well as the shifts we must make as a culture.

**LIVING THE HOPI PROPHECY**
Milt Markewitz – May 20, 2020

No problem can be solved from the same level of consciousness that created it.

Albert Einstein

**Ethical Shortfall**
*Wars, Social Injustice & Climate Crisis*

**Creating Bridges**
*Living Systems, Cultural Comparisons, Paradigm Shifts, Living Languages*

**Hierarchical Institutions**
*Business, Religion, Education & Governance are all Un-Sustainable*

**Separation From Earth**
*Developed a Human Centered Consciousness*

**Resonance Deep Inside**
*For some it was obscured, for others it was a glimpse of a reality*

**All Earth's Systems are Alive**
*Nature was our sole Mentor*

**Can only Accurately Convey the Consciousness we've Lived**
*Those who've experienced, embodied, and practiced life processes*

**Reconnect with Life**
*Nature as Primary Mentor for learning life's relational processes*

**Authentic Partners**
*Connect with local Tribes, Native schools, and support Organizations*

**Infuse Earth Wisdom**
*Valuing all life, Ecologic, Communal, Principled, Systemic, Spiritual, and Grateful*

This plan is about implementing the paradigm shift that infuses Indigenous Wisdom into our Modernity cultures. The bottom four steps lead us back to having Nature as our primary mentor and they are as follows:

1. Recognizing that only those who've embodied a specific consciousness can accurately convey it.
2. Therefore, we must develop authentic partners who will share with us what they've embodied.

3. This is the learning Modernity culture must honor and accept with gratitude to those who have graciously given it.
4. The reuslt will be a reconnection to all life and the processes and intelligence the underlies Creation and the self-organizing renewel with which we continue to be blessed.

## Plans & Processes

This book offers what we believe are the four bridges, three tools, and three plan components that guide us to change our collective state of being.

The bridges are the *Ancient Languages* that awaken a way of thinking and knowing buried deep in each of us, *Living Systems Thinking* (with the dynamics of Panarchy and Chaords) that helps us see the interrelationships and emergent properties alive in the world around us, *Spiral Dynamics* that shows how individuals, groups, and cultures evolve, and *Human Dynamics* that helps us to teach and learn regarding fundamental differences among cultures..

The three tools are the *Talking Circle* that is given to us by Earth-based peoples of the world; the *100% Consensus* process that facilitates listening and learning from each other and from Nature; and *Appreciative Inquiry* that awakens within each of us the virtues that we cherish deeply and wish to instill in ourselves, our world, and all the generations that follow.

The three plan components are: the infusion of *Earth-based ethics* into all of Modernity culture's institutions, organizations, and individuals who make critical decisions; by seeking *wisdom from Earth-based people* to guide us and help us embody what they've know for millennia; and *enrolling the multitudes of like-minded organizations and individuals* who want to return balance and harmony to our home, Earth.

To accomplish this, based on our experience and research, we suggest the following actions:

1.  **Call out to all people** who agree with, or have a listening for, the need to develop a new consciousness based on Earth-centered ethics to participate in listening and learning from and with those people whose cultures have lived in balance and harmony for generations. The networks are in place and the self-organizing exemplified by the millions of people throughout the world demanding social justice, equaliy for Women, Black Lives Matter, Democracy Now, as well as Nuclear Disarmament, and addressing the Climate Crisis. This is about 'awakening an already knowing' for modernity that is informed by Indigenous and Eastern wisdom and ethics. And as this awakening occurs it will spiral into goodness beyond what we can currently define.

2.  **Convene Indigenous and Eastern peoples** where this work is already underway and already spirit driven as they prepare for difficult times that require water, soil, food security, communal health and a clean, peaceful environment. All of this is inherently conveyed to them in their natural laws of interdependence and the ecological and communal guiding principles that govern every decision. They are relational to the core, and exemplify the relational leadership required for this process, and in addition we ask them to host ceremonial gatherings for all humanity to experience healing, reconciliation, systemic understanding, sufficient abundance, sense of place, languages, community, day-to-day survival, cooperative economics, Native sciences, and living by mutually agreed-upon guiding principles. Here we rely on Native leadership to develop the process and content, and ensure the effort is spirit-driven, and in return honor their ways with respect and fairness that is lacking by colonizing, empirical cultures.

3.  **Examine Modernity culture's unethical ways** that from an historical perepsective began with the first

empires, after millennia of humanity having Nature as a mentor and a model. It is thought that empire began shortly after the time of Abraham, and his Earth-based wisdom was compromised through enslavement and loss of language. We know Interfaith activities abound, and some are very enlightened, but too many focus on finding commonality rather than what they wish to become. They are structured to pepetuate who they are being, and many of these structures are crumbling as their congregants shift from dogmatic to more relational teachings. Leaders like Pope Francis and the Dalai Lama move us closer to examining ourselves, asking what have we wrought, and looking at ourselves to see how we devolved. Their work will be informed by the spirit-driven, relational ways of Earth-based wisdom, and the shift of the masses as they become clearer about the ethical guidance they seek from religion. And, the adoption of Earth Based ethics into all of the decisions we make with dramatically change our institutions, organzations, families, and individuals, and in turn the well-being of Earth and of future generations.

Happily, there are people currently engaged in each of these three components.:Leadership is in place, seeds have been planted and nourished, and significant sometimes massive numbers of people from all over the world have self-organized to participate in the organizations and activities that are emerging. ... and we invite you, the reader, to become part of what's happening. You can learn more about specific groups and activities on the "Awaken" page of the website: www.gaialivingsystems.org.

As you do so, we encourage you to think of them, not as discrete organizations, but as interdependent living organisms, with individual and collective emergent processes. We believe there will be a natural communications flow among them, and an ongoing synergy.

Through the implementation of these and other similar steps, we believe that ahead of humanity is the possibility of regeneration—a regeneration of individuality, liberty, community and ethics such as the world has never known—in harmony with Nature, with one another, and with the divine intelligence, just as the world has always dreamed.

# Appendix

1. The Binding of Isaac story, Revisited
2. Ruth's Releasing and Replacing Process

## The Binding of Isaac

To help quicken the recognition of characters for those not familiar with the Hebrew, we use the following code:

Cosmological characters are in a **large, bold** font;

Archetypal processes are in a medium-size font;

Existential outcomes are in a smaller, <u>underlined gray</u> font.

Prologue

As you probably know I'm known as the 'father' of the Abrahamic Traditions, and it is recognized by all that I had a very close relationship with G*d. All this is true, but perhaps not as you may think. G*d didn't speak to me in the commonly understood way that two people communicate, but instead I was in constant communion with G*d through Nature and through an energetic language that emanated from the universe and resonated with all there is. For me this is communion—relationship with all there is through mind, body and spirit. And I was not alone in that. The community from which I came also spoke this language—we were what you call mystics, and revelation abounded among us. Prior to my journey with Yitzhhaq, I had accepted the responsibility to embed a profound revelation into the genetic makeup of the generations of peoples to follow.

In brief, the revelation was an understanding that G*d's Cosmological powers create the Archetypal capacities for fertilization and birth in such a way that life can perpetuate itself in a perfectly ordered, sensually beautiful, evolutionary emergent way.

Revelation was facilitated by our Hebrew language, in which each character is a sacred geometry of sound and shape—a symbiotic energy with every other character. The language kept us deeply connected to place both locally and globally, as well as to time—past, present and future—from which emerged the ethics of how we must live each day. It was this language that informed us of our cosmology, and our responsibility to maintain the balance and harmony with which we are blessed.

It became clear to me that there are several Archetypal processes created by Cosmological powers, and it is these processes that are necessary and sufficient for the perpetuation of life. All life has been blessed with these extraordinary processes.

How was all this wisdom to be captured and passed on? I quickly realized that I must take a son to the sacred mount, *Adonoi Jireh*. Yitzhhaq–open, sensible, balanced–was my choice.

We spoke of the journey, the impending challenges, and the responsibilities. Our 4-day, 3-night journey to *Adonoi Jireh* would be physically difficult, yet our preparation was almost entirely spiritual. We initially traveled with two other men who carried some supplies, but our plan was to travel the last two days alone, during which time we would live off the blessings of this arid land.

Yitzhhaq the Potential DNA of an Enlightened People

Initially as we walked, I shared what had been revealed to me. All the while Yitzhhaq saw, heard, smelled, absorbed, and connected with everything. Then at night, with a sky filled with astrological wonder, he journeyed into the Cosmos and felt its welcome attraction.

The first night, Yitshhaq was quiet. He would ask a question from time to time, and I could feel in the silence that he was reflecting and synthesizing all that he was learning.

In the middle of the second day, we left our fellow travelers so that we could travel on alone and experience the subtle blessings that emerge from a land that otherwise looks as if it has little to offer.

That evening Yitzhhaq shared with me his understanding of the paradox of our planet, so powerful and balanced, yet so fragile. He spoke of a narrow bandwidth in which species including ourselves can live, and how we rely on *Eretz*, our Earth, to cleanse and heal. He discerned the finiteness of the planet, the possibilities of a future in which we might lose touch with the essence of life; that we might not understand that if *Eretz*, the Earth, was to take care of us then we must take care of her. He also shared that there is a spark of divinity in all of life that must be fully appreciated or we will do great harm to our environment and subsequently our social order.

We walked all day together delighted with the discoveries we were making. It seemed as if we were drawn to everything we needed. Yitzhhaq was particularly good at relying on his sensual connections to the land to intuit how to find food and water.

That night he shared with me his connection with all life, that we have all been blessed with the same basic life processes, and that we feed each other as we recompose in a life-death-life continuum. Yitzhhaq finished with the following statement,

The very essence of life has been revealed to me along with the understanding that life is not deterministic. We have choice, and with choice we have responsibilities. It is through the understanding of life that a clear ethic emerges and becomes integral to every seed. We must not lose touch with the understanding of sufficiency, and sharing that which is scarce. This knowing and way of being can only be present when we discern *Adonoi*, G*d, as the essence that resides in all life.

It occurred to me as Yitzhhaq spoke that we must never lose our symbolic language of life, or our oral tradition, because it is through the language that we are able to deeply understand the revelation.

Before we slept that night, Yitzhhaq spoke these most incredible thoughts, "I believe that I fully understand who each of us is and our relationship to the birth of a new peoples. You, 'Avraham'

| מ | ה | ר | ב | א |
|---|---|---|---|---|
| Final Mem 600 | Hay 5 | Raysh 200 | Bet 2 | Aleph 1 |

come from the Cosmic Order *(Raysh)* of life and have become the Cosmic Enlightened Human (final *Mem*), the archetype of Universal Life *(Hay)*, and living life with a complete acceptance of death *(Aleph)*. And I, Yitzhhaq,

| ק | ח | צ | י |
|---|---|---|---|
| Qof 100 | Hhayt 8 | Tsadde 90 | Yod 10 |

understand my own mission to be the seed for the generations of fully living people, *Yod*, that manifest their connection to mystery and sensual beauty, *Tsadde*, where all decisions are ethically grounded, *Hhayt*, all emanating from the Cosmic Life-Death-Life force, *Qof*. The *Yod* in my name and being flows from your *Aleph*, and the seed that I produce must not be a *Yod* that just exists, but one that lives life to the fullest by embracing and being in concert with all the blessings that are life."

I slept a wonderful sleep that night having had one of those moments of deep appreciation for my son who had transformed from being a young adult to being a peer in terms of wisdom, compassion, and leadership. Yitzhhaq had become an enlightened *Yod*, whose seed was capable of passing that appreciation of life to all the generations.

We rose early the next morning to complete our journey. We were unclear if there was to be more revelation, or how we might know if we had passed, or not passed, these most arduous and crucial tests. If we had not passed, then there could be no new people. The seed would be terminated, essentially aborted as it is in Nature if a fetus isn't prepared for birth. We were prepared for that judgment.

The cosmic forces got stronger and stronger as we approached the summit. I felt an energy the likes of which I'd never felt. I could hardly breathe, and I felt as if I was detached from my body.

I became aware of two new, very powerful, resonating forces. They were both the cosmological forces of *Qof, Raysh*.

The first, *Bikarna*, regrettably translated as 'horns', emanated from *Eretz*, the Earth. *Bikarna* is a most powerful word not only because of the Cosmological characters, but because from its two Archetypal processes Order and Impregnation emerges Existential Universal Life all part of the Life-Death-Life recomposing process.

| ו | י | נ | ר | ק | ב |
|---|---|---|---|---|---|
| Vav | Yod | Noun | Raysh | Qof | Bet |
| 6 | 10 | 50 | 200 | 100 | 2 |

The second, *Vyekra,* seemed to be coming from the heavens and is translated as a 'calling' of the angels. These two words are almost mirror images. *Vyekra* has at its Archetypal processes Fertilization and the Life-Death-Life Continuum from which emerges Existential Life-Death-Life Continuum.

| Aleph | Raysh | Qof | Yod | Vav |
|-------|-------|-----|-----|-----|
| 1 | 200 | 100 | 10 | 6 |

Both of us recognized these two forces, and as we became comfortable with them, they seemed to soften. Harmony replaced what we'd first perceived as dissonance. This final revelation was God's acceptance of Yitzhhaq as the seed for perpetuating the belief system that has become Judaism.

Yitzhhaq and I shared a simple prayer before we departed *Adonoi Jireh.* It is a prayer of thankfulness that each of us now appreciated more fully than ever before. It is a prayer each of you has often said, perhaps without meaning before, but hopefully with great meaning now. We said 'Amen', a vibrant set of shamanic characters:

| Final Noun | Mem | Aleph |
|------------|-----|-------|
| 700 | 40 | 1 |

Of all the infinite possibilities and combinations of what might be, the final *Noun* creates this beautiful Life-Death-Life Continuum... *Aleph,* we give thanks for this moment and what has been birthed... *Mem.*

## Ruth's Process

Many of my students and clients have found the following process helpful in taking the energy off of "triggers" that come up in day-to-day life. They've found that by doing these steps they experience less stress and have improved relationships, finances, and health.

1.    Awareness—seeing that something (e.g., idea, belief, situation, story, person, behavior) in our experience doesn't fit with what we know or intend our lives to be.

2.    Acceptance that such is, in fact, part of our current/past experience (rather than pretending it's not).

3.    Acknowledging that, while it doesn't at this time fit, it has served a purpose in our lives, if only to bring us to this state of being in this moment—we wouldn't be who we are today without it!

4.    Expressing the full range of feelings that come up when we look at it—literally "pushing from" our being, our bodies, our emotional center, our intellect, all the feelings, words, images, thoughts, songs, movements, that are associated with it, through writing, speaking, dancing or other movement, music, pounding on pillows, and other safe modes of expression—in a safe place away from people who might be disturbed by our doing so. We know we're done with this phase when we feel physically and emotionally drained, almost too tired and empty to do anything at all and we find ourselves saying "and I know you really were trying to love me..." or some such understanding words—sometimes we actually curl up and fall asleep at this point, or at least go into a deep meditative state.

5.    a. Releasing all of that—throwing rocks into the ocean, filling a virtual "garbage bag" and letting it be carried away or implode, burning papers, showering with intention to clean internally as well as externally, etc.–to let the subconscious mind know that the 'something' is no longer a part of our self-image. (I like stuffing it all into an imaginary rocket ship and sending it into

the sun to be transformed into healing light; one person put it in a hot-air balloon and watched it drift away; others ask angels and Christ-figures to take it away; one man's "self-consuming" bag is a delight!) We know we're done with this part when we don't feel any "charge" when we think of the people or situation.

5. b. For-giving—in that internal space of release (some folks call it "empty fullness"), imagining that each of the people involved is sitting in front of us and telling them all that we've let go of this and no longer hold them responsible for their part in it for us; imagining them in front of us we ask them to release & forgive us for resenting or blaming them, and for projecting this state or idea or action onto them; accepting that there is no blame/judgment from "on high" and stepping into a delightful "state of grace" in which "all that exists is the love between us."

6. Claiming/Declaring—in that "state of grace" is power, and we focus it to claim/accept a truer idea of our being/experience/relationship; we get to state, with clarity and feeling what we're ready to experience instead of whatever our pattern was in the past.

7. Affirming—writing and speaking this new idea frequently, practicing it, and, when any old habits of thought/action are triggered, canceling them and reminding ourselves that this new idea is how we're living our lives now.

That's it! It can take seconds, hours, days, or weeks, depending on our willingness, attachment, and focus. It's demonstrated its effectiveness hundreds of times over the 15+ years I've been using/teaching it—typically removing about 80% of whatever emotional "charge" is attached to the "something" we're experiencing.

## An Iterative, Spiral Sequence:

The feeling after completing this process is wonderful—we're free at last!

Until, some weeks or months later, we find ourselves in what seems like the same place feeling the same things. It can be really frustrating at this point, and we often think things like "I thought

I was done with this! I did that work already!" and the like. In fact, even though it may seem like we're in the same situation we were before, we're actually feeling far less upset and it lasts much less time—and if we do the process again, we can clean up another 80%, so when it comes around again we have even less to deal with!

We know we've completed the process when, one day, we realize that the "trigger" happened a little while ago and we didn't even realize it.

## The Next Rounds

After we've completed a release process for ourselves, it's interesting that most folks start hearing people around them talking about very similar issues.

When that happens, it's a great sign! It means we've done our work and eliminated it from our own life, and now it's moved out to our inner circle—so we do the process again, as if it were for ourselves, and guess what? The people around us don't have to deal with the issue any more! (This is the essence of spiritual healing and science-of-mind practitioner work.)

So we go on about our lives and next thing we know, someone is telling us about someone else who's having the same issue. So what do we do? You guessed it—we do the process as if it were for ourselves...

One of my students came in to class one day very upset: she had received an email that had been forwarded a few times from someone in Iraq describing a form of abuse that used to go on in her life. After she vented for a while I looked at her and said "congratulations! You've been doing your work well! What used to be in your face is now happening several times removed from you on the other side of the planet! Well done!" The whole class got the point.

Thanks for taking the time to explore this process. It's a synthesis of methods from a number of therapeutic approaches and has worked wonders in my life and many others, too. I hope you'll find a few hours and a safe, quiet place, gather together some paper and pencils, pens, or markers, a few pillows, and some great, expressive music and really allow yourself to feel the feelings and release them—you'll be amazed at how quickly your life begins to turn around!

~*R*

# More Useful Links & Resources

Asking the Right Questions video by Ilarion Merculieff:
https://youtu.be/GHhgZLR815M

Yakaona – Indigenous Peoples contribute to the 1992 World summit : https://youtu.be/Sy_SHwq1leo

Wisdom Keepers video: https://www.wisdomweavers.world/

Sadhguru of India meets a Lakota wiseman:
https://youtu.be/uiLdfml_rao

Willie Whitefeather's illustration of the Hopi prophecy:
https://youtu.be/VhwGScMKec4

The Case Recognize Indigenous Knowledge as Science:
https://youtu.be/X5QON5l6zy8

Indigenous in Plain Sight: https://youtu.be/s3FL9uhTH_s

We Are All Connected with Nature: https://youtu.be/xk0-yebNA_o

Native Americans: We Shall Remain:
https://youtu.be/ilf5vDptOYk

Allow Things to Unfold to Find Your Purpose:
https://youtu.be/ycB29FkoylE

Fight for Humanity: https://youtu.be/WavB4giW_S0

Patience and Tolerance: Lessons from Pueblo Traditions:
https://youtu.be/MmUPlCRdXzI

What it Means to be a Navajo Woman:
https://youtu.be/U0gCGpCtY7s

Ute Wisdom, Language, and Creation Story:
https://youtu.be/gv201ILHXhc

Indigenous Knowledge to Close Gaps in Indigenous Health:
https://youtu.be/IpKjtujtEYI

Living A Circular Life: https://youtu.be/niRs_VIqzYU

All My Relations – A Traditional Lakota to Health Equity:
https://youtu.be/3phTundagzQ

Building Resilient Communities: A Moral Responsibility:
https://youtu.be/e2Re-KrQNa4

An Indigenous Journey to Leadership:
https://youtu.be/0xxg5pJdxUY

What Aboriginal Knowledge Can Teach Us about Happiness:
https://youtu.be/Cf-dK8HFP2c

What is it Like to Be Aboriginal? https://youtu.be/9y1T3JfzRGE

True Tracks: Create a Culture of Innovation with Indigenous
Knowledge: https://youtu.be/WfS11_Dl6ew

The Myth of Aboriginal Stories Being Myths:
https://youtu.be/aUIgkbExn6I

The Value of Deep Listening – an Aboriginal Gift to the Nation:
https://youtu.be/L6wiBKClHqY

### And, directly related to this book:

www.natureslanguage.com

www.appreciativesustainability.com

www.gaialivingsystems.org/rebalanceearth

# Gratitudes – Milt

To generations past who through their connection with Nature have developed and shared the wisdom of how we can individually and collectively honor life-renewing ways. While there's no way to include all who have contributed to this effort, we thank specifically Milt's Indigenous mentors; Ilarion Merculieff who inspired so much of this book, Lewis Cardinal with the Parliament of the World's Religions, Dr Yvonne Vizina, Be'sha Blondin, Jim and Alberta Ironcloud Miller, Juan Nelson Rojas, Mindahi Bastida Munoz, Geraldine Patrick, Greg Cajete, Francois Paulette, Steve and Shawna Bluestar Newcomb, Joseph Orozco, Suzanne Thompson, James Skeet, Nancy Maryboy, David Begay, and local folks Roy Hunter Sampel, Terry Cross, Richard Twiss, JR Lilly, Patrick Eaglestaff, Cornel Pewewardy, Judy Bluehorse Skelton, Grace Dillon, Alex Merrin, Max Defender, Rod McAfey, Sheila Mitchell, Tom Schneider, Greg Archuleta, Se-ah-dom & Ed Edmo, Will Bamcroft, David West, David Lewis, Sal Sahme, Mary Lee Sumnitee Jones and her mother Marlene, Jefferson Greene, Sam and Alice Dunlop, DeVonntae Amundsen, Rose Highbear, Randy and Edih Woodley, each of the Native leaders of the American Indian Institute, the Indigenous Education Institute, the Northwest Indian College and Vine Deloria Conferences, and Wisdom Weavers of the World who shared both their pain and the wisdom that transcended that pain; folks from The Earth & Spirit Council, the Interfaith Council of Greater Portland, the United Religions Initiative, & all the other Interfaith colleagues including Michael Dowd and Connie Barlow, my recent co-workers in the Transformative Learning Foundation, Pille Bunnell, Fleurette Sweeney, Ba and Josette Luvmour, Sam Crowley, Vanessa Cabrales, Paul Freedman, Laurel Tien, and Renee Beth Poindexter, Dottie Koontz and Barbara Solomon and the IONS folks, and Lisa Smith from Pull Together Now, and other special friends who have inspired me and helped me with this work the late June Moriyasu and all her family, Marilyn Winter-Tamkin, Jeff Goebel, Batya Podos, Sheldon Hurst, Aimee

Samara, Betsy Toll, Kim Smith, Cylvia Hayes, Tammy Zinsmeister, Jean Pence, Yvonne Chang, Merle Lefkoff Anaakha Coman, Libby Roderick, Lauren Hartmann, Judith Aftergut, Georgia Marshall, Helen Spector, Catherine Crim, Ben Peek, Jerry Kasinger, Lynn Hingson, Ed and Linda Kaiel, Alan Haber, Jenny Holmes, Katherine Jesch, Kenji Stasiewicz, Emily Martin, Barbara Walden, Dennis Sandow, Bob Stensland, Tom Atlee, Heather Tischbein, Ed Smith, Patricia Martinez, Walt Roberts, Jim Newcomer, Stuart Cowan, Sally Mahe, Genevieve Chilton, Cheryll Simmerman, Emi Miller, Shiv Talwar, Matthew Sheinin, Tom Gladwin, and Joel Getzendanner; Professors Tom Johnson, Elaine Jessen, David Cooperrider, Dalton Miller-Jones, and Wayne Wakeland; and religious leaders Jan Elfers, Fr. Matthew Fox, Pastor Barbara Campbell, Imam Toure, and Rabbis Shlomo Truzman, Arthur Waskow and Hannah Laner. And last the deepest appreciation for Ruth Miller without whom I never would be a co-author, or have reflected, clarified, and enhanced my world-views.

# About the Authors

Milt Markewitz earned the MS in Whole Systems Design after retiring from a career with IBM - initially working as a programmer with a technical orientation, and soon becoming a designer of complex systems by listening and learning from cultures who honored both the aliveness of our work and the simplicity of its underlying principles. His current life-work is addressing Climate Crisis, informed primarily by indigenous wisdom traditions that have lived in balance and harmony with Earth for millennia.. Find him at:www.naturallanguages.com and learn more about his work in this interview: https://kboo.fm/media/40189-language-life

Ruth L. Miller integrates new understandings of culture and consciousness in a way that "the rest of us" can understand. With degrees in anthropology, environmental studies, cybernetics, and the systems sciences, she taught in several colleges and universities while working as a futurist and organizational and community development consultant. Now, having completed a second career as an ordained New Thought minister serving Unity, Science of Mind, and Unitarian-Universalist churches, she consults, writes, and speaks on the nature of consciousness, spirituality, and culture, focused on the future well-being of all humanity. Her website is www.ruthlmillerphd.com

2- Earth based consciousness contrasted with modernity culture.

5- hope for humanity - rediscovering & basing actions on ancient truths of living in balance & harmony w/ life renewing process bestowed on life millions of yrs. ago, then flowing w/ nature.

MODERNITY CULTURE - MC

7- condensed time line:

4.5 billion - earth formed
3.5 billion - life appeared
67 million - life processes in place today
200,000 - humans - nature is sole mentor
~~40,000~~ - for humans
~~4~~4-6,000 - human consciousness changed & no longer relied on nature as mentor
- formation of empires in fertile cres
- powerful peoples became urbanized, away from earth's process
- heirarchy became the norm & the earth became a commodity

EARTH BASED CONSCIOUSNESS - EBC

EARTH BASED NURTURE - EBN

13- can't convey earth based consciousness to those who haven't lived it. ~~E~~ 1st step is to recognize & appreciate the language & method.

19- an ethical shortfall is to ~~focus on~~ look at ourselves in the context of our upbringing - we are nurtured to become products of the modernity culture. ~~In~~ because of 41st anniversary of Mom & Dad's I've ~~took~~ reflected thru ~~earth~~ EBC & EBN - joy & faith of EBN moves me from darkness to light.

20-24 ~~xxx~~ - clarifying "philosophy of scarcity & theology of abundance". Pie chart of religions - outer ring is assumed scarcity based on modernity - divisive. Inner ring based on abundance - unifying understanding that there is more than enough to support all religions

31- earth centered cultures know earth as the source of all material wellbeing, sun is the energy for earth & the sky is the bridge.

# Related Titles from Portal Center Press

*Awakening,* a journey of enlightenment, by Andrée Cuenod

*Butterfly Soup,* a guide to changing your life (from the inside out), by Aurora J. Miller

*Discovering A New Way,* possibilities for a peaceful future in the patterns of the past, by Ruth L. Miller

*Home,* creating humanity's future, by Ruth L Miller

*Language of Life,* answers to modern issues in an ancient way of speaking, by Milt Markewitz, Ruth L. Miller & Batya Podos

*Miracles through Music,* odyssey of a harpist healer-shaman, by Joel Andrews

*Views from the Pew,* moving beyond religion & discovering truth within, by J C Pedigo and friends

*Wake Up!* our old beliefs don't work anymore, by Andrée Cuenod

**And check out our environmental fiction titles at...**

www.portalcenterpress.com

36 - EBC embraces the power of nature. The power to do so comes from the languages used by EBC around the world.

39 - The energy of some languages is every bit of & sometimes more important than vocabular

55 - ones original language is a significant determinant of how the brain is structured and works & worldview & relational being

55-6 - why change is hard but necessary.

52 - the Hopi model

60 - systemic movement from mechanical to living system: differences between the two → attributes of all living systems → the gifts to which all life has been endowed.

CPSIA information can be obtained
at www.ICGtesting.com
Printed in the USA
LVHW091600290121
677804LV00007B/242